ANTIPOVERTY HOUSEKEEPING:
THE ADMINISTRATION OF THE ECONOMIC OPPORTUNITY ACT

Roger H. Davidson

University of California — Santa Barbara

and Sar A. Levitan

Center for Manpower Policy Studies
The George Washington University

Institute of Labor and Industrial Relations
The University of Michigan   Wayne State University
Ann Arbor   Detroit

September, 1968

Copyright 1968

Library of Congress No. 6865876

$1.25

PREFACE

This study of the administration of the Economic Opportunity Act is part of a larger research project, financed by the Ford Foundation. The findings of this study will be published in *The Great Society's Poor Law*. We would like to express our gratitude to the many staff members of the Office of Economic Opportunity who took the time to meet with us and, in some cases, to read the manuscript and offer helpful suggestions. Robert A. Levine, Assistant Director of OEO, contributed many critical suggestions and technical improvements for which we are grateful, as did our colleagues, Garth L. Mangum and Mrs. Ethel W. Brandwein.

The Authors

July 1968.

CONTENTS

NEW
DIMENSIONS

The magnitude and variety of problems implied by the federal government's "unconditional war on poverty" have challenged traditional administrative theories and practices. Except on a limited scale, few people prior to 1964 had considered, let alone attempted, the functional coordination of governmental programs in American communities. The psychological and social characteristics of the poverty-stricken, moreover, demanded a heavy expenditure of manpower and money merely to identify and recruit the clienteles of the poverty programs. Even coordination at the federal level, seemingly a relatively simple task (involving primarily the funding of the efforts), is a story of frustration for those who attempted the job. Clearly, conventional notions of administrative efficiency and structure cannot be applied to the organization of the antipoverty programs.

Because the problem of poverty permeates many aspects of our national life, the administration of poverty-related programs has stretched traditional jurisdictions of public institutions. The programs are funded by a number of federal agencies but are normally administered by state and local agencies. But much of the money which Congress appropriated for the first three years of programs under the Economic Opportunity Act was never entered on the ledgers of state and local governments, but rather was spent by nongovernmental entities— a feature of the Act which proved controversial as well as innovative. At the community level, nonprofit organizations worked individually or cooperatively to plan and implement poverty programs, occasionally without an elected office-holder in sight. Not surprisingly, research and demonstration grants were made to educational institutions and a diverse array of other research organizations. And private firms acted as contractors for such tasks as running Job Corps centers. Here again, traditional notions of the lines which divided public and private institutions seemed outmoded.

LEVELS OF ADMINISTRATION

The Federal Level

Though the Office of Economic Opportunity spends only a small portion of the federal antipoverty dollars, it was envisioned in the Economic Opportunity Act as the nerve center of the federal government's antipoverty efforts. OEO is a unique administrative organization. For certain programs—urban Job Corps centers, Community Action, VISTA, and migrant workers—the agency has operating responsibilities. This alone would set OEO apart, for it is actually located in the Executive Office of the President—a status usually reserved for staff or advisory agencies. Other programs under the Economic Opportunity Act, however, are delegated to other federal departments or agencies, including the Departments of Labor (Neighborhood Youth Corps), Agriculture (part of the Job Corps Conservation Centers and rural loans), Interior (the balance of the Conservation Centers, except for a few which are operated by states), and Health, Education, and Welfare (adult basic education and work experience), as well as the Small Business Administration (small business loans). Finally, OEO is charged by a vague mandate with coordination of federal poverty-related programs which are not a part of the Economic Opportunity Act.

OEO's operating responsibilities were the result of specific compromises during the legislative history of the Act. The agency's position in the Executive Office, as well as its potential role in coordinating programs not under the Act, were included in the original bill at the insistence of R. Sargent Shriver—head of the Administration's task force and Director of OEO during its first three and a half years, the time span covered by this study.

These features are reflected in OEO's organizational structure (Figure 1), largely the product of preliminary planning during the summer of 1964. The top levels of the chart reflect staff functions, some traditional and others specifically designed to serve OEO's unique mission. The four assistant directors (third line in chart) are responsible for direct administration of programs charged to OEO. The final level of OEO organization, the seven regional offices, was a later development.

It is apparent from the legislative history of the Economic Opportunity Act that no overall rational plan dictated either the selection of programs to be included in the Act or their distribution between the new OEO and federal agencies already in the poverty business. The distribution was essentially pragmatic, involving two sets of factors: existing agencies' expectations that they would "get their share" of the new program, and the preferences of Shriver and his associates, backed by the President.

The Secretary of Labor received something less than he had hoped for, in view of his department's long-term interest in manpower problems and its responsibilities under the Wagner-Peyser Act (United States Employment Service), the Manpower Development and Training Act, and other legislation. Labor's share was the Neighborhood Youth Corps, administered by the Bureau of Work and Training Programs in the Manpower Administration. Though somewhat less aggressive in bargaining, the Department of Health, Education, and Welfare wound up with three important poverty programs: the Work Experience and Training Program, administered originally by the Welfare Administration and since 1967 by the Social and Rehabilitation Service; and the adult basic education and work-study programs, both administered by the Office of Education and transferred formally to HEW within the first two years of the legislation. Rural antipoverty loans are administered by the Farmers Home Administration in the Department of Agriculture, while financial assistance to small business comes from the Small Business Administration's revolving fund. Because the Act places the authority for the administration of all EOA programs with the Director of OEO, the delegation of these programs can, in theory, be rescinded by him.

OEO's own operating programs reflect Shriver's interests

and his distaste for traditional welfare activities. VISTA, the domestic peace corps, was a natural extension of Shriver's experience with, and enthusiasm for, the Peace Corps. The Job Corps held hopes for spectacular accomplishment (its administrative perils were not anticipated), and Shriver decided to run it himself, overriding the objections of the Labor Department. Finally, the Community Action Program represented the kind of coordinating operation which OEO, as a staff agency, was particularly designed to handle. However, CAP has tended to break down into specific-purpose programs, ranging from birth control to creating jobs for old people. The goal of coordinating programs in aid of the poor remains largely elusive. Figure 2 shows both the direct and delegated programs based on the 1967 amendments.

Practically every activity which OEO attempted to fund was already preempted or claimed by an established federal agency. Even the neighborhood centers, supposedly a CAP creation, had antecedents in the settlement houses, though these were rare. More significantly, newly-funded neighborhood centers partially duplicated well-established single purpose centers–Employment Service offices and health clinics, to mention two of the most frequently available services. The Job Corps was a relatively distinctive program that might be well run by a new agency with a minimum of duplication of existing activities: there were previously only a few residential facilities (outside of "reform" schools and penal institutions) providing remedial education and training for poor youths. But even here problems of coordination soon appeared. What, for example, was the Job Corps' relation to the Neighborhood Youth Corps? What criteria should be applied in selecting youths for the Job Corps as compared with the Neighborhood Youth Corps–not to mention the various counseling and training programs funded by the Departments of Labor and Health, Education, and Welfare? A coordinated attack on poverty would presumably involve some form of "one-stop" counseling and referral service to evaluate the needs of disadvantaged youths and direct them to appropriate programs. Yet even when a single agency–the U.S. Employment Service–was assigned to recruit enrollees for youth programs, selection remained largely on a haphazard basis, and coordinated referral was rarely achieved. The problem of coordinating poverty-related programs was heightened rather than alleviated by the addition of OEO's new programs.

The problem of coordination may never be "solved," if only because the problem of poverty is likely to continue to demand a variety of institutional stratagems. With the proliferation of related programs, coordination becomes ever more burdensome for officials and clienteles alike; and in many cases the distinctions between programs are—to borrow the words of one bureaucratic memorandum on the subject—"largely artificial and arbitrary."

Different interests, of course, generated different approaches to the problem. The Labor Department, long unhappy at the thought of having other agencies in the manpower field, was more convinced than ever that all work experience and training programs should be placed under its own protective care. Labor was especially concerned about the profusion of agencies in its fields, and about what it called the "urgent need . . . to rationalize the entire manpower development structure." Quite a different solution for the proliferation of manpower programs was proposed by the National Association for Community Development (NACD) at its December 1965 convention. Composed largely of community action agency officials, NACD urged that, wherever possible, manpower programs be folded into the CAP operations. The community developers recommended specifically that OEO give higher priority to manpower programs within the CAP concept, and that:

> Presently fragmented programs (adult literacy, work experience, Neighborhood Youth Corps) be understood and funded as integral parts of a comprehensive manpower program . . . . It is through the community action mechanism that such essential resources can be effectively integrated with existing manpower and occupational training programs.[1]

The differing positions of the Labor Department and the CAP workers were only indicative of the vast scramble for advantage among the many interests involved in poverty programming.

In the manpower field, OEO's efforts at coordination at the federal level have been, for the most part, fruitless. The agency initially lost influence over the Neighborhood Youth Corps

(NYC), and its efforts to reclaim some measure of control met with frustration. With the addition of the Nelson-Scheuer and Kennedy-Javits manpower programs in 1966, OEO agreed to delegate these programs to the Labor Department—with the proviso, however, that funds for these projects would be allocated through local community action agencies. OEO hoped to strengthen these agencies and recoup some influence over NYC by including it as part of the interagency agreement. OEO officials were apprehensive over this agreement (concluded early in 1967), but most thought it was the best way out of a difficult situation. Moreover, involvement of CAA's gave further promise of coordination at the local level.

A related effort was the Concentrated Employment Program (CEP) to create jobs and train slum residents in 20 cities and two rural areas. CEP's funds came from MDTA and three EOA programs. In most areas the CAA's were given the prime responsibility for implementing the projects, or at least the grants were funneled through these agencies.

Congress itself stepped in and attempted to force coordination of Title V projects by requiring HEW to share responsibility with the Labor Department for providing work experience and training to public assistance recipients and other needy persons. This coordination, however, was slow to materialize. With the 1967 legislation, Title V was to start phasing out—its functions being largely absorbed by a new work experience and training program for relief recipients, enacted as part of the 1967 amendments to the Social Security Act.

Early in 1967, OEO and four federal departments involved in administering manpower programs—Labor, HEW, Commerce, and HUD—signed a "treaty" to establish the Cooperative Area Manpower Planning System (CAMPS). The results of one year's experience were not promising, but hope springs eternal.[2]

The problem of coordination was not limited to manpower programs, though the problem was more visible in that area because of the Economic Opportunity Act's stress upon training, work experience and job creation. Coordination also proved a problem in funding health and education projects. Neighborhood health centers, funded by CAP under a 1966 amendment sponsored by Senator Edward M. Kennedy of Massachusetts, were an attempt to provide comprehensive medical services for some communities, linking various publicly-financed (federal, state and local) health programs. In the educational sphere, co-ordination between OEO's Head Start and the Title I programs of the Elementary and Secondary Education Act threatened to become a glaring deficiency. As an early and popular venture of CAP, Head Start underwent a rapid expansion which was ac-complished with little intervention from the Office of Educa-tion. Later enactment of the Elementary and Secondary Educa-tion Act and subsequent efforts to establish Follow-Through programs to supplement Head Start, however, made formal co-ordination imperative. The two agencies therefore signed an agreement delegating Follow-Through to the Office of Educa-tion even before Congress had authorized the program. The advance planning proved premature when Follow-Through be-came a victim of "economy" and only one-eighth of the re-quested funds was allocated for the program during fiscal 1968.

The problem of coordinating poverty-related programs at the federal level is closely tied to the question of which pro-grams OEO should administer itself and which should be "spun off" to other agencies. The original legislative package drew this line rather arbitrarily. Since then, two programs—Work-Study (1965) and Adult Basic Education (1966)—have been spun off from the Economic Opportunity Act; and OEO's friends and foes alike have from time to time proposed further transfers which they claim would result in a more "logical" or "efficient" operation. OEO has withstood these attacks upon its programs, a fact confirmed in 1967 when Congress refused to tamper further with OEO's operating responsibilities. In opposing the proposed transfers, OEO claimed that its overall coordinating functions would be weakened and the antipoverty efforts would suffer by removal of programs from EOA.

Under the Economic Opportunity Act, OEO's responsibil-ities for coordination were extended beyond the programs initi-ated by the Act. The authority given to the Director of OEO is broad but lacks political muscle. Various sections of the Act provide, as James L. Sundquist phrases it, "statutory basis for OEO's role as Government-wide coordinator of antipoverty ef-forts." [3] These provisions charge OEO's Director with "co-ordination of antipoverty efforts by all segments of the Federal Government"; establish a Cabinet-level Economic Opportunity Council chaired by the OEO Director; empower the Director to obtain data and reports from other agencies; authorize the Director to create an information center for all federal antipoverty programs; and require all agencies to give "preference" (within certain limits) to projects which are part of CAA programs.

Implementation of these mandates clearly hinged on the aggressiveness of the OEO officials and the tolerance of program administrators in other agencies. Not surprisingly, therefore, OEO exerted little effort to fulfill its government-wide role, and other agencies in turn were not anxious to call attention to the deficiency. For its part, OEO became preoccupied with day-to-day administration of its own programs, devoting attention to non-OEO programs "only as [it] became necessary to the implementation of the programs for which it was responsible." [4] OEO at first sought to meet the problems of coordination by creating an Office of Interagency Relations. Though its primary mission was supervision of delegated programs under the Economic Opportunity Act, the Office broadened its functions to embrace all interagency relations as well as OEO's links with local and state governments. The mission of federal-level coordination remained amorphous, and in 1967 the title of the Office was changed to "Office of Governmental Relations."

The statutory body charged with coordinating functions—the Economic Opportunity Council—has proved ineffective. Because other agencies tended to consider the Council a creature of OEO, they did not view it as an ideal forum to air problems or resolve differences. Top officials rarely attended, leaving the Council in the hands of underlings. OEO's Office of Governmental Relations provided staff assistance for the Council, and OEO Director Shriver chaired the meetings. But, by all accounts, Shriver did not rely heavily upon the Council as an instrument of influence. In 1967, therefore, Congress approved an OEO-sponsored amendment giving the Council its own staff. By freeing the Council from OEO ties, it was hoped to lend it more legitimacy in the eyes of the other participants. By May 1968, the Executive Secretary of the Council had not yet been appointed.

If OEO is viewed as a coordinating agency, a "command-post for the war on poverty," its record must be viewed with skepticism. However, the task of coordinating federal programs is a mammoth problem which pervades many program areas—whether in poverty, or health, or education, or, for that matter, foreign affairs. The Senate Subcommittee on Employment,

Manpower and Poverty noted in 1967 that a "constant theme" of its field hearings and consultant studies was "the lack of effective coordination among Federal programs." [5] If this is the case—and all evidence points to this conclusion—then the problem is far too wide and persistent for OEO to resolve on its own, with the weak resources at its command.

Regionalization

OEO approached the matter of regional offices with considerable caution. First, the agency wanted to develop confidence in its procedures, and until then, final authorization for all projects rested in Washington. Second, additional staff would be required, and toward the end of fiscal 1965, OEO was feeling the effects of a Congressionally-imposed ceiling on personnel.

Because OEO was in part a coordinating agency, an important question was where the regional offices were to be located. During the summer of 1965, with the active encouragement of the Budget Bureau, the agency held a series of meetings with representatives from Labor and HEW with a view to establishing common regional boundaries. The question could not be resolved because existing departments and their component bureaus had for a number of years proliferated regional and local offices. But the discussions themselves were fruitful, one result being OEO's creation of seven regional offices paralleling those of the Labor Department's Neighborhood Youth Corps.

By September 1965, Shriver was ready to announce a broad policy of "decentralization," though he revealed no details of the plan. From that time on, however, grant applications for CAP-funded projects were handled increasingly in the regions, with most of the processing of papers being done there. This became possible as OEO's guidelines proved to be workable. Meanwhile, OEO's regional staffs were augmented to prepare for the process of decentralization. Of the three OEO operating agencies, CAP was the first to decentralize.

In December 1965, the planned decentralization of CAP was announced by OEO. Officials in Washington retained review of applications for research and demonstration grants and conduct and administration grants for the very largest of the urban CAA's. Based on early experience, OEO estimated that 90 percent of all grants could be approved at the regional level. However, big-city applications tended to be more complex packages, and OEO officials did not feel they could delegate these to the regional offices.[6] Later, OEO pushed the decentralization of CAP even further; there is now no dollar limit on grants which can be approved by the regional offices, though OEO officials in Washington still urge that problem cases be referred to them and sometimes appear unwilling to yield full authority to the regions.

Community action operations are the most decentralized of OEO's activities. Regionalization of CAP administration occurred with relative ease because procedures were geared to decentralization from the very inception of OEO. On the other hand, OEO's decision to include most CAP grants in its decentralization was especially significant because these programs tended to generate the largest measure of controversy from local officials. Moreover, there were numerous reports of local mismanagement of CAP funds—in Boston and New York, for example. In light of the potential controversiality of these projects, OEO's willingness to decentralize its review procedure was especially courageous. In addition to review, the regional offices were also delegated the functions of inspection and civil rights compliance. Here again, the delegations were significant in view of the Washington staff's "hard line" reputation for requiring that projects meet stringent standards.[7]

Other OEO programs were slower to decentralize, and some officials resisted the agency's efforts at regionalization. The Job Corps, for example, was operated on a national basis from the beginning and, as of late 1967, had decentralized very little. VISTA, too, was operated nationally at its inception and was slow to regionalize. VISTA officials argued that national administration was needed because of the need to clarify the objectives of their program, and the uniqueness of the volunteers' role in the war on poverty. By late 1967, however, slightly more than half of VISTA personnel were in the regional offices. These officials were given total responsibility for project development, recruitment of volunteers, in-service training, and field support of volunteers. Headquarters and field staff share responsibility for training VISTA volunteers. Originally, the migrant workers program operated directly out of Washington, and it has continued to do so.

Several types of review were established for regional operations. First, there was a review process in the field similar to that handled by the headquarters during OEO's first year. Regional offices added personnel—principally lawyers, civil rights specialists, and auditors—to perform these functions. Secondly, uniform processing systems were established; and personnel exchanges, orientation programs, and field trips by Washington personnel were encouraged to enhance uniformity. Third, OEO headquarters established a grant review branch within CAP to perform a post-review of CAP grants. A sample of CAP applications is sent to Washington for review as a kind of "quality control."

An early, tangible result of regionalization was the fact that the grant process was shortened considerably, with OEO aiming eventually at a 60-day cycle from application to funding. When backlog problems developed, OEO responded by adding personnel to the regional offices. By mid-1967, regional offices accounted for 39 percent of the 2,700 persons on OEO's permanent payroll. There was little variation in the size of staff among the seven regional offices, which ranged from 153 to 186 (including temporary personnel) at the latest available count.

The States

The states occupy an inconspicuous position in the Economic Opportunity Act. As drafted by the Shriver task force and as passed by Congress, the Act was clearly designed to give the new OEO maximum flexibility in dealing with state, local, or private organizations. This flexibility was intentional. Many of the Administration officials who had a hand in drafting the measure foresaw that certain governors, for policy or political reasons, might try to sabotage the objectives of the antipoverty program. (One member of the Shriver task force recalled that whenever the role of the state was discussed, the name of then-Alabama Governor George C. Wallace would be mentioned and the discussion would promptly terminate.) A more fundamental reason for excluding the states was that the community action concept, which many saw as the crux of the new law, implied that the states were not relevant for more than an advisory or supportive role. President Johnson himself appeared to give credence to this notion by speaking repeatedly of local initiative and asserting that the problems of the urban environment "require us to create new concepts of cooperation—a creative federalism—between the National Capital and the leaders of local communities."[8]

It would be a mistake, however, to conclude that the states did not play a role in the EOA programs—even before enactment of the Green amendment in 1967. CAP funds, though allocated directly to communities, are distributed among the states on the basis of: (a) number of public assistance recipients in the states; (b) average number of unemployed; and (c) ratio of children in families with an annual income of less than $1,000. OEO may reserve up to 20 percent of the total funds for distribution in accordance with criteria of its own design. In the HEW-administered programs of Title V, the state welfare agency has to approve the project proposal and provide overall supervision even though the local welfare agency runs the day-to-day operation. In other programs, the states (as well as localities) are eligible to become contractors—for example, six Job Corps conservation centers are operated by state agencies. And where standards for such professional personnel as teachers or social workers are involved, state licensing practices inevitably come into play. The problems of interlevel cooperation are extremely complex, but they have been marked not so much by permanent state-federal fixtures as by the more complicated adjustments required to mesh programs to the many and differing state laws, practices, and personnel.

Technical assistance has provided a particularly hopeful avenue for state participation in the war on poverty. Under the Act, OEO's Director is authorized to contract with state agencies for technical assistance to localities in developing community action programs. By the end of 1967, every state had established its own antipoverty headquarters—usually called the state "Office of Economic Opportunity." (One state, Indiana, later closed its office.) The federal funds used to create these offices were by no means large (ranging from $5 million in the first year to $7 million in 1967), but they were undoubtedly well spent. State technical services were especially valuable to rural communities, which often lacked the indigenous leadership and expertise to develop CAA's and consequently fell behind the better-organized urban areas in procuring federal funds. In speaking to the Governors' Conference in mid-1965, Shriver stressed that:

> Too often, it has been the big cities that have been able to get the federal money first—because they can attract the experts—because they know how to put together a staff attached to the mayor—and they know the arts of grantsmanship.[9]

After generations of complaints that state governments have favored rural areas at the expense of the cities, one of the larger ironies of the "war on poverty" has been the rescue operation which the states performed for rural areas which were ill-prepared to engage in planning and implementation of federally-backed programs.

State technical assistance offices could perform other functions. For example, Shriver called upon the states to encourage research and to stimulate multi-county and metropolitan anti-poverty efforts. When the governor appointed a capable person as poverty coordinator and gave him sufficient authority to act, the results were often promising. New Jersey's Governor Richard Hughes devoted particular attention to his poverty program, and OEO officials subsequently pointed out that New Jersey obtained a great variety of OEO grants. The New Jersey OEO actually administered an NYC program, made extensive use of VISTA volunteers in migrant programs, and generally coordinated the development of CAA's in the state. In California, the state coordinator's office stimulated a broad-gauged migrant program featuring day-care and educational programs, overnight camps and sanitary facilities, and the use of transportable housing for migrants at the height of the growing season. Several other states can boast of equally productive contributions to the poverty campaign.[10]

Unfortunately, the gubernatorial veto issue at first threatened to overshadow all other phases of the states' role. The Administration's 1964 draft bill on poverty required gubernatorial consent before VISTA volunteers could be dispatched to that state. In the community action programs, OEO's Director was admonished to "facilitate effective participation of the states" and to refer project applications to the state's governor for "comment." Before passing the Act, Congress considerably strengthened the hand of the governors by amending the bill to include—in addition to the veto for VISTA projects—a governor's veto of Job Corps centers and all contracts with non-governmental agencies (including community action agencies).

Governors saw the veto as an important weapon, not only for coordinating poverty efforts, but for insuring that their own political position would not be jeopardized by policies and "patronage" associated with the programs. It was this latter objective that caused the most bitter disputes between OEO and state officials, provoking a number of threatened vetoes and its actual use on five occasions during the first year of the Act. The most publicized veto came when Governor George C. Wallace of Alabama turned back OEO funds which had been allocated to a bi-racial poverty group in Birmingham.[11] Because of its racial overtones, Wallace's action was influential in leading Congress to reconsider the whole question.

The Administration's proposed 1965 amendments to the Act failed to mention the governor's veto, but the Wallace incident provoked immediate debate on Capitol Hill. A coalition of Republicans and southern Democrats in the House insisted on retaining some form of the veto, and in the final version of the amendments the governors were permitted vetoes over Neighborhood Youth Corps, Community Action, and Adult Basic Education projects. The veto was merely a token power, however, for the OEO Director was permitted to reverse the veto, if he wished.[12] States' rights forces, while successful in blocking complete deletion of the provision, were never deluded into thinking their victory had been anything but a Pyrrhic one.

Nevertheless, even the diluted veto power gave some governors an opportunity to assume a public stance of fighting "waste and extravagance" by OEO in order to earn political capital. Altogether, ten states used 30 vetoes, or one for every 550 grants made by OEO during its first three years. Governors Wallace of Alabama (both George and Lurleen combined) and Ronald Reagan of California were the champion vetoers, accounting for three of every five vetoes.[13] Governor Reagan's actions received the greatest public attention. An examination of his veto record indicated, however, that the ten vetoes he exercised during his first year of office accounted for less than one percent of the total funds allocated by OEO to California; and some of the projects he vetoed became effective after expiration of the 30-day waiting period. However, it might be misleading to measure the impact of the veto merely in terms of the magnitude of funds involved or the percentage of total approved grants. The veto power's propensity to draw attention to questionable or controversial projects may have served to persuade officials to modify their program applications or to prevent OEO approval of certain projects.

The veto question generated considerable publicity and no doubt was symptomatic of very real frustrations on the part of state officials. Nonetheless, though the formal veto has been eliminated for most practical purposes, the states retain a wide variety of potentially significant functions in the war against poverty. What is obvious to date, however, is "the unclear definition of the role of the states" in EOA efforts.[14] Nor is there any consensus of their future role. State officials and their supporters, of course, call for a greater voice in poverty programs. But local officials tend to be suspicious of state involvement. "The State agencies, even when they do not become involved in a local urban program," remarked Detroit's Mayor Jerome Cavanagh, ". . . lack either the interest or the sophistication or the understanding of the immediacy of the problem."[15] The ultimate place of the states in the EOA programs will depend, therefore, upon further developments in the system of federal relationships.

The Local Level

The Economic Opportunity Act is innovative in its approach to federal-local relations. The community action concept envisions comprehensive and community-wide planning and implementation of programs aimed at combatting poverty. The institutional vehicle at the local level is the umbrella-type "community action agency," a public or private nonprofit agency designed to pull together a locality's existing institutional resources and to develop its "community action program," a functional agenda for its needs in fighting poverty. Responsibility for administration of existing programs normally remains with established agencies, and CAP-funded activities may be taken over by the CAA or delegated to other institutions, public or private.

The community action concept is intended to restructure

social services in several ways. First, from the standpoint of the federal government, the multi-purpose CAP is an alternative to the traditional special-purpose grant-in-aid, and in this respect approaches the concept of the block grant. Only local planning, it is reasoned, can account for unique local needs; and these needs cannot be met by a plethora of federal agencies sponsoring their own specialized grant programs. The levers for pulling together federal resources are found in two preference provisions in the Act which direct OEO and every other federal domestic department to assign highest possible priority to proposals of CAA's. Understandably, therefore, the Bureau of the Budget displayed an early interest in CAP as a device for coordinating federal programs and by-passing traditional jurisdictional lines.

Second, the community action concept envisions coordination at the local level, since CAA's are supposed to be broadly representative of community opinion in matters relating to social welfare. Thus, it was with considerable casualness (surprising only in retrospect) that the drafters of the Act specified (Section 202[a][3]) that CAA's be "developed, conducted and administered with the maximum feasible participation of residents of the areas and members of the groups served."

A third aspect of the CAP concept is its functional approach to geographic and political boundaries. Though CAA's frequently parallel existing political boundaries, the concept is open-ended in permitting these boundaries to be crossed for practical purposes in planning or implementing poverty programs. This development is not without significance, in view of the proliferation of governmental and political jurisdictions—especially in complex and even multi-state urban regions. In addition, contiguous rural counties occasionally coalesced to form one CAA.

The vast majority of the 1,050 CAA's funded during OEO's first three years proceeded with a minumum of administrative difficulty. OEO provided initial funds to develop a program and to finance the cost of organizing and hiring staff, and only a few communities refused to accept the "tainted" money. In most of these cases, the CAA was simply an administrative framework for the kinds of work which community agencies had already been doing; and most of the funds undoubtedly were channeled directly to what OEO called "the local welfare system"—that is, schools, welfare agencies, local charities, etc.

Most CAA's, moreover, enjoyed at least the tacit support of

local governmental officials. In urban areas, a mayor's task force typically set the process in motion, although a coalition of civil rights, welfare, and related groups sometimes served the same function. Rural areas, lacking the institutional base of their urban counterparts, typically relied on private organization or agricultural extension service agents to organize CAA's. From OEO's point of view, city hall cooperation was valuable in providing needed access to local governmental funds and facilities. Under the Act, a portion of the CAP funding must come from the locality—although this may be "in kind" contributions, such as staff time. Originally this local contribution was set at ten percent, but in 1967 Congress raised the figure to 20 percent—though, to the great relief of local poverty officials, it killed a proposal that local contributions be in cash. OEO guidelines also specified that CAA's be able to mobilize existing local "service systems," such as schools and welfare agencies.

From the vantage point of city hall, too, cooperation had its payoffs. Most local officials preferred to exercise some control over the direction of CAA's, though some found it convenient to pursue a policy of calculated distance—namely, exercising informal direction of the CAA's while appearing to grant independence. Many local officials, nonetheless, soon found the autonomous CAA's a threat to their authority and their control over local jobs. The U.S. Conference of Mayors, for example, endorsed the original poverty bill with the reservation that CAP funds be channeled through an official agency such as a local human development corporation. The National Association of Counties took a similar position, and Mayor William F. Walsh of Syracuse went so far as to observe that " . . . if we could not have direct control of the program we would not want it."[16] At one point the bill's House sponsor, Representative Phil Landrum (D-Ga.), promised to "draft language" to assure inclusion of local governments; but the original bill was never altered in this way. For the first three years, the community action concept remained free of formal requirements for the involvement of local politicians and officials.

As the CAA's got underway, however, it became apparent that their relationship with local government was inherently "uneasy and sometimes strained. . . ."[17] On the one hand, localities were eager for federal money, and such bodies as the National Municipal League and the U.S. Conference of Mayors gave the war on poverty strong support. On the other hand, many local officials—particularly in large cities and throughout the South—feared that CAA's would organize the poor (and the Negroes) to upset traditional political power alignments. Thus spokesmen for local governments, such as the Conference of Mayors, continued to insist that "the key decision-maker in the selection of a board to plan the city's community action program is the mayor, as the chief local elected official."

For three years OEO walked a tightrope on the issue of city hall or county courthouse involvement. The agency's objectives—particularly participation by the poor themselves—could sometimes be achieved only by flying in the face of the community's traditional social prejudices or political arrangements. Thus, one agency directive called for the rejection of CAA's "set up in a manner calculated to ensure domination by a single individual or organization." Political pressures, however, proved too powerful to prevent incursions upon the autonomy of CAA's. By March 1966, OEO was informing its regional offices that city or county elected officials could veto all or any portion of a CAA proposal. The OEO directive stated:

> There may be occasion where no community action agency may be better than one with the veto power resting in a prejudiced local government.

> Our policy is to accept a veto where this will produce community action. This policy does not mean that we must accept a veto where the effect will be to prevent community action.[18]

Though militants were inclined to view this move as a sell-out, OEO officials defended it as a response to political realities. When asked about the action, Bernard L. Boutin, then Deputy Director of the agency, explained that "concurrence" of local officials was sought in certain communities "where it is the best part of prudence in order to get a program going."[19]

In 1967, Congress curtailed the autonomy which the Economic Opportunity Act had originally conferred on the CAA's. With Adam Clayton Powell removed as chairman of the House Education and Labor Committee, House Democrats were free to explore means of saving the embattled poverty program by making it more palatable to hostile politicians. The vehicle was the so-called Green amendment—its original sponsor was Representative Edith Green of Oregon—which considerably re-defined the CAA concept. This amendment, voted by the House and accepted somewhat reluctantly by the Senate, required that CAA's be designated by state or local governments. The CAA itself might be an agency of the state or local government, or a nonprofit (public or private) agency designated by them. In the event that the state or local government failed to create or designate a CAA, or failed to submit or carry out a satisfactory CAA, the OEO Director was authorized to select a nonprofit organization as the CAA. Whatever the character of the CAA, it was required to have a governing board not exceeding 51 members and divided equally among three groups—public officials; democratically-selected representatives of the poverty areas; and representatives of business, labor, civic, and charitable groups (Sections 210 and 211 of the 1967 Act).

The Green provision was attacked as the "bosses and boll weevil amendment" because it neutralized opposition to OEO among southern and big city Democrats and became a major factor in the 1967 extension of EOA. The extent to which the amendment has impaired the CAA's as instruments of social change is, however, a major question which cannot be answered for some time to come. Clearly, the amendment does violence to the original CAA concept. Yet, at least two things may be said in behalf of the change. First, in the long run, it is probably desirable for CAA's to draw closer to local governments. Second, the CAA's role as lobbyist for social change, while undoubtedly impaired, is nonetheless not precluded under the newer arrangement.

OEO's interpretation of the Green amendment and the guidelines for its implementation[20] drew attacks from diverse groups, including the U.S. Conference of Mayors, the National Association of Counties, the Citizens Crusade Against Poverty, and many others. Mrs. Green herself was reported to have ex-pressed dissatisfaction with OEO's guidelines, charging that the agency misinterpreted the spirit of her amendment and watered down the responsibility of elected officials for administering CAA's. She claimed that OEO was continuing "business as usual."[21] OEO spokesmen, recognizing "the wealth of prob-lems" inherent in the Green amendment, anticipated "small wars among political jurisdictions. . . . The big issue will be which politicians grab control."[22] It would require unusual skill for OEO to avoid entanglement in these local and state struggles and to escape unscathed from these battles. A final judgment on issues raised by the 1967 amendments will be an important aspect of any future assessments of OEO's accomplishments.

Footnotes

[1] Recommendation of Manpower and Employment Conference, National Association for Community Development, December 1965.

[2] A discussion of CAMPS is found in Garth L. Mangum, *MDTA: Foundation of a Manpower Policy,* (Baltimore: The Johns Hopkins Press, 1968), pp. 71-75.

[3] James L. Sundquist, "Issues of Organization and Coordination," U.S. Congress, Senate Committee on Labor and Public Welfare, Subcommittee on Employment, Manpower and Poverty, *Examination of the War on Poverty, Staff and Consultant Reports,* 90th Cong., 1st Sess., (Washington: Government Printing Office, 1967), Vol. III, p. 787.

[4] *Ibid.,* p. 788.

[5] U.S. Congress, Senate Committee on Labor and Public Welfare, Subcommittee on Employment, Manpower and Poverty, *Economic Opportunity Amendments of 1967,* Report 563, 90th Cong., 1st Sess., (Washington: Government Printing Office, 1967), p. 6. A fuller discussion of manpower coordination is presented by Sar A. Levitan and Garth L. Mangum in *Making Sense of Federal Manpower Policy,* Policy Paper No. 2, Institute of Labor and Industrial Relations, The University of Michigan–Wayne State University (Ann Arbor, Michigan: The Institute, 1967).

[6] Office of Economic Opportunity, *Community Action Memo 15,* January 11, 1966.

[7] Robert Walters, "Poverty Agency Shifts Power to Regional Units," *The Washington Evening Star,* December 9, 1965.

[8] Commencement address at The University of Michigan, Ann Arbor, Michigan, May 22, 1964. A discussion of "creative federalism" is presented by Roger H. Davidson, "Poverty and the New Federalism," in *Dimensions of Manpower Policy*, Sar A. Levitan and Irving H. Siegel, (eds.), (Baltimore: The Johns Hopkins Press, 1966), pp. 61-80.

9 Address of R. Sargent Shriver at Governors' Conference, 57th Annual Meeting, Minneapolis, Minnesota, July 28, 1965.

1 0 For evaluations of technical assistance agencies in seven states, see U.S. Congress, Senate Committee on Labor and Public Welfare, Subcommittee on Employment, Manpower and Poverty, *Examination of the War on Poverty, Staff and Consultant Reports,* 90th Cong., 1st Sess., (Washington: Government Printing Office, 1967), Vol. VIII.

1 1 Ray Reed, "Wallace Vetoes a Poverty Grant," *The New York Times,* May 13, 1965.

1 2 *Congressional Record* (Daily Edition), August 17, 1965, pp. 18888-9 (Senate) and September 15, 1965, pp. 23073-8 (House).

1 3 *Congressional Record* (Daily Edition), October 4, 1967, p. S14147.

1 4 Terry Sanford, "Poverty's Challenge to the States, *Law and Contemporary Problems* (School of Law, Duke University, Winter 1966), p. 7.

1 5 U.S. Congress, Senate Committee on Labor and Public Welfare, Subcommittee on Employment, Manpower and Poverty, *Examination of the War on Poverty, Hearings,* 90th Cong., 1st Sess., (Washington: Government Printing Office, 1967), Part 1, p. 104. For an opposing view, see Paul Ylvisaker's testimony, pp. 138-157.

1 6 U.S. Congress, House Committee on Education and Labor, *Hearings on Economic Opportunity Act,* 88th Cong., 2nd Sess., (Washington: Government Printing Office, 1964), Part 2, pp. 822 and 790.

1 7 See Footnote 10, Vol. III, pp. 801-2.

1 8 Robert Walters, "Mayors Can Have Veto Over Poverty Programs," *The Washington Star,* March 23, 1966.

1 9 Eve Edstrom, "Powell Would Halt War on Poverty Rather than Give Veto to Mayors," *The Washington Post,* March 28, 1966.

2 0 Office of Economic Opportunity, *Organizing Communities for Action Under the 1967 Amendments,* February 1968.

2 1 Eve Edstrom, "OEO 'Guide' Is Blasted on 3 Fronts," *The Washington Post,* February 14, 1968.

2 2 Jonathan Spivak, "Poverty Planners Fear Program's Switch to Public Control May Spur Bitter Battles," *Wall Street Journal,* February 12, 1968.

STAFF
SUPPORT

Because of its publicized claims to the position of command-post for the nation's scattered poverty programs, OEO is likely to be judged ultimately not only upon its performance of operating functions but also upon its performance of supporting, or staff, functions—coordination, planning, evaluation, research, and generating interest in poverty problems. In the realm of coordination, OEO has responded by creating two unique administrative organs. The Office of Governmental Relations has already been alluded to. Another unique creation, OEO's Office of National Councils and Organizations, is designed to handle the agency's relations with the "outside world" and will bear examination later in a different context. In addition, OEO has developed some fresh approaches to the problems of research and evaluation which merit consideration at this point.

Planning and Research

OEO's Office of Research, Plans, Programs, and Evaluation (RPPE) is charged with the long-range responsibilities implied by its title. Joseph A. Kershaw, the Williams College Provost who first headed this office, described it as ". . . a RAND Corporation in the poverty program . . . a facility to study the long-range problems of poverty in a basic, as opposed to an operational, sense." This ambitious job description fit in with the "cost effectiveness" concept, first introduced on a large scale in the Department of Defense and later spread throughout the federal establishment. The research staff under Kershaw and later under Robert A. Levine took the leadership among federal agencies in applying systems analysis techniques to welfare efforts. Drawing on the vast supply of pertinent statistics, the RPPE staff classified and quantified the various sub-universes of the poverty population, analyzed the applicability of existing welfare programs to these groups, and prepared complementary and alternative plans for combatting poverty.

Regrettably, the findings of RPPE remain largely in the files of the "Poverty House" (as OEO's headquarters is known), though some have been transmitted to the Bureau of the Budget. Since the work was part of the regular five-year planning cycle in which government agencies engaged, it was withheld from the public under the cloak of "executive privilege." During the course of the 1967 hearings on the Economic Opportunity Act, Senator Joseph S. Clark, chairman of the Senate Subcommittee on Employment, Manpower, and Poverty, tried unsuccessfully to obtain the products of OEO's planning. The following exchange took place:

Senator Clark. ...I think there must be something definitive in this record which would show any overall plan or any overall strategy as to how you would hope by 1976 to win this war against poverty...This phobia with executive secrecy is doing the poverty program no good on the Hill...We on this subcommittee are entitled to know as a matter of right what your overall plan and strategy is for winning the war on poverty...

Mr. Shriver. Mr. Chairman, if we give something to the Bureau of the Budget, that is no longer our document. It is their document, not ours.

Senator Clark. Let's be candid about that. You keep carbon copies.

Mr. Shriver. Yes, but that is not our document. When I send you a letter, when you receive it, it's your property. There is a copy of our letter, and I don't release it.

Senator Clark. Would that that were the general rule in politics. [Laughter.]

Mr. Shriver. That is the general rule at OEO.[23]

Public information about significant RPPE work is limited to a few sketchy newspaper reports—the result of "leaks," either inadvertent or contrived. Neither Congress nor the public, therefore, may ever have an opportunity to assess OEO's proposed programs from the vantage-point of OEO's own research findings.

While RPPE's basic function was planning strategies to combat poverty, it became involved in more mundane matters. The office underwent three distinct phases of emphasis during its first three years of operation. During OEO's first few months, RPPE activities were largely confined to developing the agency's budget for fiscal 1966. In doing so it filled a vacuum produced by OEO's lack of regular staff for budgeting. This activity also reflected the interest of the Acting Director, Leon Gilgoff, who had served as Associate Budget Director for the U.S. Air Force before joining OEO. When Kershaw took over in June 1965, he emphasized long-range planning and divorced RPPE from operational responsibilities. In these early stages of OEO, RPPE took seriously the mandate of planning a "total war on poverty" based on the assumption of steeply increasing resources for waging the war. Even in the face of escalation of the other war, Kershaw continued to develop his plans; and as late as the summer of 1966, Shriver still anticipated that poverty could be eliminated by 1976, the 200th anniversary of the Declaration of Independence. His prediction was based upon RPPE estimates that the job could be done "merely" by doubling the total federal outlay for antipoverty efforts. By the time Kershaw left, 14 months after he assumed office, it became quite clear that the domestic war would have to be delayed. Instead of expanding antipoverty programs, OEO in 1967 was fighting for its very life. In this atmosphere, there was no need to refine its grandiose planning, and RPPE shifted its concern to operational research, evaluation of on-going programs, and planning for these programs within the serious budgetary constraints. The grand designs of 1965 and 1966 were kept in the files, awaiting more propitious times.

In addition to in-house research, RPPE's mission included basic research into the dimensions of poverty and existing programs to combat it. Under an early contract, a research institute prepared a catalog of existing federal poverty programs. RPPE also helped design evaluations of programs and projects initiated under the Economic Opportunity Act. For example, several universities were given funds to evaluate in depth CAA programs in their immediate vicinities. Possibly the most significant project undertaken by RPPE was funding an Institute for Poverty Research at the University of Wisconsin to undertake "fundamental and applied research into poverty." In this case, RPPE played a "seeding" function by financing the Institute during its formative years, with the University accepting responsibility for continuing the effort once OEO support expired.

Another significant RPPE-funded project—reflecting the widespread interest in income maintenance schemes—provided for field study to investigate the impact of graduated work-incentive payments upon the lives of the poor. The $4 million demonstration project provided a three-year study of a sample of 1,000 urban families, including some who would receive income support and a control group to whom payments would not be made. The project, Robert A. Levine anticipated, will shed light upon the feasibility of "providing income support for those normally excluded from welfare. . . the working poor."[24]   The experiment was to be conducted by a private research firm in six New Jersey cities.

Information Centers

As originally conceived, RPPE's mission included development of OEO's operational statistics and the broader task of compiling data on distribution of all federal antipoverty programs and expenditures. In the fall of 1965 these functions were separated from RPPE and placed in a new Information Center. In the rhetoric of OEO, this Center was described as "the national center room for the war on poverty." A number of factors contributed toward the creation of the Center. Gilgoff, who as *de facto* director of RPPE before Kershaw assumed office had gained the status of a major advisor to Shriver, was felt to deserve responsibility for a separate office. Kershaw, who preferred to concentrate on long-range planning, welcomed the opportunity to divest himself of day-to-day operational responsibilities. There was also a substantive rationalization for the separation of the two offices: it was felt that operating agencies might be reluctant to have operational data in the hands of RPPE, whose function was to review and evaluate their programs.

A major achievement of the Information Center was development of the Federal Information Exchange System—which included catalogs of federal poverty programs, community profiles, and federal expenditures by county and by type of classification, particularly concentrating on poverty programs. Such a need might appropiately have been met by the Bureau of the Budget, but that agency took no steps to perform the function. As head of the Information Center, Gilgoff stressed development of this information as part of OEO's interest in overall federal antipoverty efforts. Though he set up the system for the development of these data, he regrettably died before the project was completed.

The Information Center was less successful in the more immediate task of gathering, collating, and disseminating current information about EOA programs. In part this was due to its over-ambitious plans for developing a complete "systems approach to EOA efforts." The Center might have succeeded had it settled for traditional statistical data relating to the characteristics of the persons served by the several programs, allocation and distribution of project funding, follow-up on program participants, and related questions. Some officials wanted data which would provide longitudinal measures for effectiveness of EOA programs. When Head Start was initiated, for example, there were some who advocated a follow-up on Head Start participants to permit measurement of the impact of the program. Since more than half a million children were enrolled during the first summer of the program, the task was quite evidently beyond the capacity of the Center's limited resources. Several months elapsed before OEO gave up on this effort, but meanwhile precious time and resources were wasted.

Lack of effective communication and cooperation from OEO operating agencies and the administrators of delegate programs was an equally serious obstacle to the development of operational data. Not surprisingly, program administrators insisted upon maintaining their own operational statistics and were not cooperative in feeding the necessary data to the Information Center's computers. The Job Corps developed its own statistics independently. CAP experienced a different set of problems. Most of the newly organized CAA's placed low priority on collection of data and failed to report on program operations, except to the extent required by law to show accountability for expenditures. In addition, a major portion of CAA funds was assigned to delegate agencies, many of which were neither accustomed nor inclined to submit operational reports to the CAA's. Head Start projects, which were administered mostly by local school systems, offered an excellent illustration.

The Work Experience and Training administrators in HEW's Welfare Administration faced yet another set of obstacles. Accustomed to making grants to states and delegating to state officials the responsibility for administration of programs, they were not very successful in getting projects or the welfare agencies to cooperate in regular and complete reporting of their activities. The Neighborhood Youth Corps did not develop a satisfactory reporting system during its first three years and therefore had little data to feed to the Information Center. Friction developed early between the Neighborhood Youth Corps and Information Center, each agency maintaining that the other was responsible for developing the data; by the summer of 1967, NYC set up its own information system independent of the Information Center.

Underlying all the difficulties was a failure to develop, much less agree upon, program goals—a prerequisite to the development of the PPBS concept. In the absence of clearly set goals, technicians found it difficult to design measurements of program achievements.

Office of Inspection

The seemingly thankless task of checking complaints and halting incipient scandals is handled by OEO's Office of Inspection. Such an office appeared to be worthwhile political insurance with programs as fraught with potential controversy as those handled by OEO, and this reasoning undoubtedly led Shriver to borrow the concept he had originally developed in the Peace Corps. William F. Haddad, who as first head of this division had the pretentious title of "Inspector General," described his activities as an "early warning system." Because Haddad and his staff of investigators had authority to investigate any EOA project at any time, however, other OEO officials soon labeled it the "fink shop."

Various complaints pour into OEO offices. Many are baseless, a few are not. In either case, investigation is needed to determine the facts. First, an initial examination must be made to ascertain whether there are any grounds to the complaint. If preliminary checking indicates that field study would be advisable, an investigator—perhaps a former news reporter or an investigative lawyer—may be sent to the scene.[25] In view of the nature of this function, it is hardly surprising that many of OEO's operating officials grew to resent such "snooping." Since Haddad reported directly to Shriver, other administrators were often uninformed of his forays before they actually took place. As one former OEO official lamented, "I had operating responsibilities, but Haddad had the power to stir up everyone." In part as the result of opposition both outside and inside OEO, Haddad left his job in late 1965. The title, "Inspector General" was dropped, and Edgar May, a Pulitzer prize-winning newspaperman and author of a popular book on poverty,[26] was appointed to the job.

Under May's leadership, the Office of Inspection began to function as a confidential reporting service for OEO officials. "This office should neither be seen nor heard, except by the people responsible for the programs," May explained. "I see this not as a spy operation [for Shriver], but as a continuing service to the operating officials." Aware of the criticism of Haddad's operation, May was careful to check with OEO operating officials or regional directors before initiating investigations. In addition, findings were reported to the OEO Director only after they had gone to the responsible official. In part as a result of this change of style, the Office of Inspection had an increasing number of requests for studies from officials within OEO.

No doubt the Office of Inspection was a fortunate addition to OEO. Much has been said about the "scandal-prone" character of OEO programs, and indeed there are many reasons why the antipoverty programs should be expected to receive controversial press treatment. In this perspective, the really impressive fact about OEO programs was how *few* damaging scandals actually resulted.[27]

The Search for Personnel

The recruitment of competent personnel is a crucial task for any agency, and especially for one starting its work *de novo*.

Unlike many new agencies, OEO had no organizational base in the federal government, except for the hastily-created Shriver task force. In the summer and fall of 1964, therefore, the recruitment problem was a challenge and a peril for OEO: if a capable, enthusiastic, and creative staff could be put together, it might be able to shape the new agency's mission unencumbered by notions left over from prior organizations. Without a staff of such quality, however, the new agency could flounder badly—no matter how promising its mission might be.

A new agency needs several distinct types of personnel to operate effectively. Most importantly, it must have administrators who are capable of taking an expansive view of the agency's mission while maintaining its political relations with the White House, Capitol Hill, and other federal agencies. Second, there must be technical specialists who are familiar with the policy problems with which the agency is concerned, and who are able to supply information and insights in implementing these policies. Third, any agency has need of "old government hands"—people who are at home in the bureaucratic habitat of Washington and who are familiar with traditional relationships between the Executive and Legislative branches, and among the federal bureaus and agencies. Finally, and not least importantly, capable clerical and supportive personnel must be found—a not inconsiderable task even for established agencies.

If this personnel problem were not formidable enough, OEO additionally faced an unfavorable manpower situation. The paradoxical task of launching an antipoverty effort in a time of booming economy meant that potential poverty warriors were in short supply. A tight market prevailed especially for skilled professional and clerical workers. Moreover, the "poverty profession"—if it could be called that—was not exactly an established one in 1964. Since no one had ever attempted a coordinated attack on poverty, it was not clear exactly what skills would be necessary, or where they could be found. The conventional professions—social work especially, but also sociology, economics, public administration, and political science—were obviously relevant, but personnel in these fields were already in short supply. And since many of OEO's planners apparently believed that professionals in these fields had already failed in dealing with poverty, it was not a settled question whether these professions had anything to offer the new enterprise.

As with many of its administrative policies, OEO's approach to personnel—at least at the top levels—was highly colored by the views of Shriver, its first Director. Shriver had helped his brother-in-law recruit top-level officials during the early days of the New Frontier, and from all accounts he never lost his zest for recruiting people. His experience both in and out of government had provided Shriver with two distinctive and related beliefs about personnel: a faith in the "inspired amateur" and a consequent acceptance of frequent rotation among high-level personnel.

Shriver himself was something of an amateur in government. Before he arrived in Washington in 1961 to organize the Peace Corps for his brother-in-law, President Kennedy, Shriver had broad experience in the fields of business and education. In planning the Peace Corps, Shriver utilized a barnstorming task force composed of educators, businessmen, labor leaders, churchmen, and others. Shriver often recalled that most experts in foreign affairs were distrustful of the Peace Corps idea. Yet, he noted, "The world is better off because the amateurs, those who had faith and trust in mankind, did not listen to the experts, who had lost both!"[28] The Peace Corps experience demonstrated to Shriver that intelligent and concerned amateurs could succeed where experts had failed—by demonstrating their interest, getting close to the people with whom they were dealing, and applying common sense. And in the Peace Corps a variety of persons were drawn upon to give leadership to the new program.

Shriver took an identical approach to OEO. Of course, he could not delude himself with the assumption that no one had ever fought poverty before, any more than he could have believed that no one had tried foreign aid prior to the Peace Corps. But his enthusiasm sometimes gave this impression. Again and again during his first year as OEO's Director, Shriver stressed the revolutionary characteristics of the war on poverty. Radical changes in structures and techniques, he repeated, would be required to succeed in this "new enterprise." A variety of experts and skilled technicians must bring their insights to bear on the problem, but no group or profession had a monopoly of information. Such talk of a "new personnel" was not calculated to please social workers who felt that they had been fighting poverty for many years, and the theme was repeated in too many speeches to be dismissed as anything less than a deep-seated disdain for the so-called professionals. To be sure, it was not long before Shriver was led to concede that he could not combat poverty without the professionals; but his basic faith in the creativity, the combined skills, and the simple humanity of the "inspired amateur" was unabated.

Businessmen, as a special species of "inspired amateur," were especially attractive to Shriver. His affinity for businessmen seemed to be a composite of several considerations. For example, he seemed to believe that a high salary was a rough indicator of a man's worth. If men on whom the business world had conferred a high price could be induced to join OEO at a considerable financial sacrifice, this fact might convince skeptics of the "soundness" of the antipoverty efforts. Thus Shriver appeared often to recruit with an eye to the press release which could be issued on the man's appointment. Persons from other professions, where pay scales were not as high, were in this viewpoint less attractive—since their tour of government duty would not represent as great a financial sacrifice.

Measured by these standards, many of the men brought in by Shriver were impressive "catches." In some cases, however, men were induced to leave their jobs and join OEO when there were no specific functions for them to perform. A former Shriver associate told of the plight of one such man, a successful businessman lured to Washington by the prospect of fighting the war on poverty at Shriver's side. The businessman showed up at OEO, and a subordinate official had to call Shriver to ascertain what job the man was to perform. "Oh, I don't know," Shriver replied. "Why don't you set up a series of interviews so he can go around and see people." According to OEO officials, this was not an isolated incident.

If personnel were to be recruited broadly from the ranks of private life, it followed that they had to be accepted for short-term assignments. There were several reasons for this. First, if they were successful in their chosen professions, they were likely to be unwilling to endure the financial sacrifice of government service for an extended period of time. Secondly, their employers were often eager to get them back. Finally, if not settled in a career, the person tended to be a restless individual, eager to shift to a new venture once the initial excitement of the poverty war had worn off. For these reasons, the people desired by Shriver were likely to accept only short-term assignments.

Shriver seemed to consider such turnover a positive blessing. In his view, turnover (within limits) was beneficial to an organization: the possible dangers of discontinuity in policy were more than outweighed by the constant infusion of new ideas. Thus a really good man could enter the agency, make his contribution, and leave the agency better for it.

Whatever benefits could be claimed for high turnover, OEO paid heavily to obtain them. Turnover was most functional during the period of the Shriver task force and during the first few months of OEO's existence. There were no precedents, and the need was for fresh ideas and creative planning. But as soon as the agency turned to implementing its programs, the "inspired amateur" often proved inept. OEO's coordinating functions, for example, demanded personnel who could promise a degree of continuity. Familiarity with governmental procedures, as well as time to master intricate problems and establish rapport with counterparts in other agencies—these qualities were badly needed by OEO and not always forthcoming. Continuity was also desirable in OEO's relations with clienteles in the field, especially the local CAA's. Officers of local CAA's sometimes complained that they had started to negotiate with a given OEO official in developing a project idea; but by the time the project was submitted for funding, the original OEO official was no longer on the scene. Particularly as the agency grew and developed its own precedents, new employees, no matter how bright and capable, required months to learn the ropes. Often they left the agency just as they began to be most useful to it—a phenomenon which may have contributed to their own education, but probably at some cost to OEO.

Lack of continuity was particularly damaging in the post of Deputy Director—the official responsible for OEO's internal administration. Indeed, the position did not acquire continuity until the appointment of Bertrand M. Harding, an able federal administrator who came to OEO in June 1966 and later succeeded Shriver as head of the agency. A variety of factors may have been responsible for the rapid turnover of deputies and the periods of vacancy in the office. But the point is that continuity was lacking in a crucial position in which continuity was essential.

The extremely fluid group known as the "Shriver task force"

did not go out of business once the Administration's draft bill was completed in March 1964. It continued to work throughout the spring and summer, attempting to plan the structure and procedures to be used by OEO once the agency was created. The group also helped to sell the bill on Capitol Hill and was able to provide House and Senate committees with technical advice. Many in this group remained with OEO.

In one important instance, an early political decision was reached which deprived OEO of a man who was reputed to be a highly talented administrator. Adam Yarmolinsky, on loan from the Office of the Secretary of Defense, had served as operating head of the Shriver task force and was slated to be named OEO's Deputy Director. Yarmolinsky was anathema to many southern Congressmen, for as Special Assistant to Defense Secretary Robert McNamara he had helped draw up a 1963 directive aimed at halting off-base discrimination against Negro servicemen stationed in the South. The Administration felt it needed Southern votes for the Act, and a number of powerful Southerners pressed Shriver to sacrifice Yarmolinsky. So Shriver gave the word, enabling floor manager Phil Landrum to announce on the floor that "I have been told on the highest authority that not only will he not be appointed, but that he will not be considered if he is recommended for a place in this agency."[29] It seemed a necessary concession at the moment, but it left a vacancy in the OEO hierarchy that was not filled until seven months after the Act was signed.

In April 1965, Jack Conway, the highly-respected director of AFL-CIO's Industrial Union Department, was chosen for the job which Yarmolinsky would have held. In the intervening months, the gap in this key position may have been responsible for some of OEO's operating difficulties.

The delay in appointing a Deputy Director was especially damaging because, during OEO's first year and a half, Shriver retained his earlier job as Director of the Peace Corps. Shriver maintained offices (linked by a "hot line" phone) in both agencies, attempting to shuttle between them and allocate time to the two operations. Although in this initial period Shriver was popular on Capitol Hill, there was recurrent Congressional criticism of the dual arrangement. Senator Winston Prouty of Vermont, for example, complained that "the poverty army is led by a part-time general."[30] Shriver's response to the criticism was that the decision lay with the President. "Both positions are Presidential appointments," he told one reporter. "It's his responsibility to decide whether the jobs are being done."[31] Finally, in early 1966, the President appointed a new Director of the Peace Corps to succeed Shriver.

OEO's top leadership was drawn from a variety of sources. Many were experienced federal bureaucrats; others came from business, education, state and municipal government, journalism, social work, and the labor movement. The sources of OEO's "supergrade" personnel (top three grades of the federal Civil Service) and Executive appointments, as of November 1967, are shown in Table 1. As can be seen, a solid majority of OEO's leaders at that point had been recruited from the federal government—from other executive agencies or the legislative branch. There is reason to believe, however, that these figures somewhat understate OEO's reliance upon non-federal personnel during the first three years. By the time these figures were compiled, many of OEO's original officers had left to return to private life, to be replaced from the ranks of governmental personnel. As the agency matured, therefore, it probably tended to recruit more of its top personnel from within the federal establishment. Among these personnel, too, a change in OEO's practices apparently occurred during the three-year period. To replace the original wave of "outsiders," OEO at first turned to proven administrators from other federal agencies; later the agency tended to promote from within its own ranks.

Table 1
Source of OEO Top Officials
November 1967

Total	51
Federal government	31
Business	9*
Local or state government	6*
Education	4
Other	2

*One person appears in both these categories.
Source: Office of Economic Opportunity.

As would be expected, turnover was high during OEO's first three years. As Table 2 reveals, separation rates in the agency during this period never dipped below 50 percent; and for two of the years they hovered around 60 percent. It is true that these figures tend to exaggerate the turnover of OEO personnel; they include all employees, and terminations for all reasons. The figures also reflect OEO's extensive use of part-time and full-time consultants during most of this period. (As of June 30, 1965, temporary staff constituted 17 percent of the total.) Nonetheless, the figures give some indication of the instability of OEO's personnel.

Table 2
OEO Separation Rates, 1964-1967

	Fiscal 1965	Fiscal 1966	Fiscal 1967
Gross separation [a]	60%	51%	59%
Controlled separation [b]	n.a.	n.a.	19%

[a] Includes permanent employees, temporary employees and consultants, as reported to the Civil Service Commission.

[b] Excludes separations of temporary employees, as well as retirement, military service, relocation, maternity, and schooling.

Source: Office of Economic Opportunity.

In OEO's highest positions, turnover was particularly high. Of the 24 top posts in OEO, all but four had experienced turnover by November 1967; and in some jobs there had been three or four incumbents. Of the four positions which had not turned over, two had been created long after the agency itself. Thus only two men—Shriver and Donald M. Baker, the General Counsel—had been in their posts from the inception of OEO; Shriver himself left in April 1968. Nor do these figures give the full story, for in many instances jobs went vacant for extended periods of time or were in the hands of acting directors.

OEO's rate of turnover occasioned considerable comment. Frequent newspaper articles—no doubt based on fragmentary or exaggerated impressions—pointed to the number of staff vacancies and implied that the war on poverty was on the brink of disaster. OEO spokesmen explained that the vacancies did not represent internal policy disagreements or personality clashes, but that they were entirely anticipated because many officials had been recruited on a temporary basis. Nonetheless, the impression remained that the turnover rate—whatever its origins—was inordinately high and that OEO's programs suffered as a consequence.

The recruitment problem was not confined to top or middle management. During these years Washington, like many other communities, was suffering from an acute shortage of clerical help. "My biggest problem in the fall of 1964 was finding clerical personnel," recalled William Kelly, OEO's first administrative chief. Kelly therefore inaugurated an intensive search for qualified secretaries, and in time OEO concluded that it was no worse off then other federal agencies in finding secretarial help.

OEO's personnel problems were compounded by legislative and administrative ceilings on personnel. During the summer of 1964, the Shriver task force attempted to reach personnel projections for the various phases of EOA. By the end of the summer it was decided that approximately 1,150 people would be needed to run the OEO's Washington office. But a far larger number of OEO's personnel would be located not in the agency itself, but rather in the Agriculture and Interior Departments for administration of the Job Corps' rural conservation centers. OEO's total projected personnel needs for fiscal 1965 amounted to 4,520 persons. Ignoring these projections, the House Appropriations Committee had attached a personnel ceiling of 4,000.

By the summer of 1965, OEO was becoming cramped by the ceiling because of growing staff demands of Job Corps conservation centers and the planned strengthening of OEO's regional offices. Accordingly, OEO requested removal of the personnel ceiling. This change was effected without difficulty, but it did not occur until October 31, 1965, because OEO's budget requests came in a supplemental appropriations bill.[32]

OEO had to live with ceilings upon its own personnel, exclusive of the Job Corps conservation center workers. These levels were set by the basic legislation (for fiscal 1965) and then by Budget Bureau estimates (for subsequent fiscal years). Table 3 compares these ceilings with the actual "on-board" staffing for each year (as of June 30 of each year). The figures demonstrate OEO's tendency to rely heavily upon temporary personnel—including consultants and part-time personnel. They also suggest that, although the personnel ceiling for the initial year of OEO's operations was not constraining, subsequent ceilings soon became so as OEO expanded its operation for implementation of its various programs.

Table 3
OEO Staffing Levels, Actual and Ceiling

Fiscal Year	Total	Permanent	Temporary
1965 (actual)	1,306	616	690
1965 (authorized)	1,350	1,150	200
1966 (actual)	2,840	1,947	893
1966 (authorized)	2,150*	2,150	—*
1967 (actual)	3,111	2,684	427
1967 (authorized)	2,950	2,800	150
1968 (authorized)	3,020	2,870	150

*A monetary limitation of $1.111 million was placed on temporary personnel for Fiscal 1966.

Source: Office of Economic Opportunity.

One final aspect of the personnel question needs to be mentioned. Critics of the poverty program regularly charged that OEO was hiring too many high-priced personnel. Republicans on the Senate Labor and Public Welfare Committee, for example, pointed out that one of every 18 OEO employees was of "supergrade" status, a figure which compared favorably to most other federal agencies.[33] On other occasions critics produced figures or lists purporting to show the high salaries of the poverty warriors.[34] Finally it was charged that salary schedules of CAA's were unduly high, often considerably above those of local or state officials performing similar functions. In 1966, Congress reacted to the "getting-rich-by-fighting-poverty" charges by limiting federal contributions to local community employees to a maximum of $15,000 a year; local funds had to be used to pay salaries above that amount and could not be counted as part of the ten percent local contribution. This amendment was one of Congressman Powell's contributions to the war on poverty.

Without defending each and every personnel decision made by OEO, it must be observed that this was not one of the more provocative charges made against the agency. It is true that OEO had no shortage of supergrades on its payroll, and that CAA salaries were often generous (though hardly extravagant). But several features of OEO's personnel needs must be reiterated. First, a ready labor force of poverty warriors simply did not exist at the time OEO was setting up shop. Secondly, the skills most relevant to the war on poverty were already in short supply. Finally, it would be misleading to compare OEO's proportion of high-grade personnel with those of other agencies. As a coordinative and administrative agency, OEO would be expected to have a larger proportion of high-level personnel than an agency—the Post Office or Defense Departments, for example—which includes large numbers of relatively low-paid operatives.

The tight labor market for such personnel as the antipoverty programs demanded also accounts for some imbalances at the local level—though it is relevant to note that salaries for local and state personnel involved in the poverty program (in community action agencies, for example) are set in the first instance by the localities themselves and not by OEO. And if there are imbalances in comparison to local and state civil service rates, this does not necessarily mean that the poverty program's salaries are out of line. It is quite likely, in fact, that the program would be utterly unable to obtain qualified personnel if it were tied to local civil service rates.[35]

Footnotes

2 3 See Footnote 15, Part 9, pp. 2711-2.

2 4 "On Relief, Wages, Jobs," Letter to the Editor, *The Washington Post,* February 2, 1968.

2 5 For accounts of the inspection function during Haddad's tenure, see Joseph A. Loftus in *The New York Times,* August 1, 1965; and Walter Pincus in *The Washington Evening Star,* August 11, 1965.

2 6 Edgar May, *The Wasted Americans* (New York: Harper and Row, 1964).

2 7 "Poverty Program: Dim Issue," *The Christian Science Monitor,* June 22, 1966.

2 8 Address at the National Conference on Poverty in the Southwest (Tucson, Arizona), January 25, 1965.

2 9 *Congressional Record* (Daily Edition), August 5, 6, 7, 1964, pp. 17610-52; 17672-739; 17932-18025.

3 0 U.S. Congress, Senate Committee on Labor and Public Welfare, *Economic Opportunity Amendments of 1965,* Report 599, 89th Cong., 1st Sess., (Washington: Government Printing Office), p. 68.

3 1 Richard L. Lyons, "Shriver Says Hot Line Helps in Peace Corps, War on Poverty," *The Washington Post,* April 27, 1965.

3 2 Public Law 89-309, October 31, 1965.

3 3 See Footnote 30, pp. 59-60.

3 4 *Congressional Record* (Daily Edition), July 28, 1965, p. A4157, and August 18, 1965, p. 20076.

3 5 U.S. Congress, House Committee on Education and Labor, *Examination of the War on Poverty Program,* 89th Cong., 1st Sess., (Washington: Government Printing Office, 1965), pp. 30-2.

OEO AND
ITS CLIENTELES

Few agencies have as wide and varied contacts with public and private interests as the Office of Economic Opportunity. In addition to dealing with agencies at all levels of government, OEO engages many private or quasi-private interests, lobbies, and professional and civic organizations. These multiple relationships, which emanate from the agency's programs and from the Economic Opportunity Act itself, have been alluded to previously. It remains, however, to detail the institutional devices OEO has developed to maintain these relationships.

Church-State Relations

Those who drafted the Economic Opportunity Act foresaw the difficulties of defining the role of sectarian institutions; and in fact this was one of the most thoroughly discussed issues during Congressional consideration of the war on poverty. For the Shriver task force, the basic policy constraint was the Kennedy Administration's position on church-state relations, embodied in a 1961 memorandum from the General Counsel of the Department of Health, Education, and Welfare and growing out of the long-standing controversies over federal aid to education. The memorandum held that *general* aid to sectarian institutions was unconstitutional because—as with elementary and secondary schools—it would be impossible to separate sectarian and nonsectarian activities. Federal programs should therefore be administered by public agencies, though they must be open to students from parochial schools.

Working in cooperation with HEW officials who were knowledgeable about the school issue, the Shriver task force's drafting team adopted this "shared time" concept for Title II of the Administration's bill. After intensive negotiations, Congressmen and Shriver's staff reached an acceptable compromise which provided for "special remedial non-curricular" programs which could be administered by either public or private schools.[36] Fortunately as it turned out (a task force charged with defining "special remedial non-curricular aid" soon became hopelessly bogged down), this provision was deleted in the final version of the Act. The final wording in Title II was left entirely open-ended concerning the recipients of aid, requiring merely that "no grant or contract . . . may provide for general aid to elementary or secondary education in any school or school system." (Section 205[b])

The church-state issue was somewhat more easily dealt with when, as in the work-study programs of Title I, institutions of higher education were involved. Under the Senate amendment which found its way into the final version of the Act,[37] there was no prohibition against grants to sectarian colleges and universities. However, student work projects under the program could not involve the "construction, operation, or maintenance of so much of any facility as is used or is to be used for sectarian instruction or as a place for religious worship."[38]

OEO's officials soon evolved a complicated set of guidelines controlling church participation. Their caution, however, did not prevent several outside groups, including the New York Civil Liberties Union and the American Jewish Congress, from questioning whether the restrictions were sufficient or whether they were being effectively administered. A single law suit, challenging the constitutionality of church participation in Head Start projects in Kansas City, Missouri, was filed but later withdrawn.[39]

In general, the churches have had a growing, and largely happy, relationship with the antipoverty programs. Criticism of the type previously mentioned has been exceedingly rare. And for their part, the churches have increasingly broadened their sense of mission in such social issues as poverty (not to mention civil rights). Church-related groups have been active participants in such programs as Head Start, Neighborhood Youth Corps, and Title III migrant labor programs. Antipoverty programs have been granted extensive and sympathetic coverage by many religious publications. In early 1966, leaders from Protestant, Catholic, and Jewish faiths formed the Interreligious Committee Against

Poverty. "Our opposition to involuntary and unnecessary poverty," the group announced, "is deeply rooted in theological convictions which are shared by our three religious communities."[40] This group was able to provide liaison among religious social action organizations, and between these organizations and OEO. Many of the religious leaders associated with these bodies were also found on the rolls of such organizations as the Citizens Crusade Against Poverty.

The Welfare Professionals

As we have already mentioned, OEO was at first conceived as independent of the "welfare professionals" who had traditionally dealt with the needy and the unskilled—educators, training specialists and social workers. However well-intentioned the traditional welfare programs had been, Shriver and many of his associates seemed to believe that they had stagnated in the hands of the professional associations and state agencies which controlled them. Moreover, these groups were accused of having "captured" some bureaus in the Department of Health, Education, and Welfare which were charged with implementing national programs.

Consistent with this attitude toward the "professionals," the poverty warriors at first seemed to want to strike out on their own. Their independence was stressed repeatedly in speeches calling for new blood in the administration of welfare services. Particularly conspicuous was an extemporaneous speech which Shriver presented on May 27, 1965, to 5,000 social workers at an Atlantic City convention of the National Conference of Social Welfare. "There are many," Shriver declared, "who think working with the poor is their own exclusive province." He went on to assert that "they"—which was taken to mean the professionals—resented any questions about their programs or salary scales. "I wonder how many people in our city slums protected welfare workers and building inspectors during last summer's riots," Shriver said.[41]

This kind of hostility could not realistically continue. Whether OEO liked it or not, existing organizational and personnel resources were firmly in the hands of the so-called professionals. Of necessity, OEO found many of its dollars going to the same interests which had been administering the more traditional programs. Who, for example, was to implement Head Start or in-school Neighborhood Youth Corps? In most cases the only available resources lay in the hands of the local school boards, and it was they who contracted with CAA's to do the job. As in its relationships with local governments, OEO found inevitably that it could not live without the professionals. In fact, the two problems were more than analogous since in many cases the welfare professionals were enmeshed with local and state governmental agencies.

OEO soon created an unofficial work group to facilitate liaison with the welfare professionals. The official peace overture, however, came in December 1965, in a speech by Shriver to 2,000 social workers at the biennial conference of the American Public Welfare Association in Chicago. Declaring that OEO had "new weapons" against poverty, Shriver said: "We want you to use them. We want your help."[42] Terming himself only a "recruit" in the antipoverty field and saying that he was making his appeal "humbly," Shriver sought to placate the social workers by calling for higher salaries and more welfare spending generally.

OEO's change of direction was largely a matter of attitude and rhetoric. In reality, OEO had dealt with the welfare professionals from the very beginning; but as one OEO official expressed it, the agency's "early actions were sometimes combative." Feeling that these traditional groups had failed the poor, OEO officials apparently believed they could teach these groups to do the job properly. These same officials would subsequently argue that the later "soft line" policy represented no fundamental change of thinking. What was being done earlier, they maintained, was merely to stimulate the social work fraternity into greater awareness of the problems of poverty and the limitations of earlier approaches. Whether OEO succeeded in this intended role is certainly open to question. What is beyond question, however, is that OEO could not live without the welfare profession and that it soon realized this fact.

Business and Labor Groups

One of the most intriguing aspects of OEO had surely been its acceptance by a significant portion of the business community. Businessmen's long standing coolness toward federal welfare programs did not necessarily apply to the EOA programs; on the contrary, many have been eager to respond to Shriver's appeals and enlist in the effort. In 1965 and 1966, for example, a United States Chamber of Commerce task force produced several studies on poverty of which one OEO official said: "Except for a few minor details, this could have been written word for word by the AFL-CIO."[43]

This friendly spirit could not have resulted merely from Shriver's undisguised admiration of businessmen or his persistent efforts to woo them to his cause. As David K. Carlisle of Litton Industries, and active early contractor in the program, explained it: "We got into the poverty war for two reasons. One was the opportunity to serve the community. The other, the business opportunity."[44] The two reasons were equally important.

The business community of the 1960's was more socially conscious and receptive to welfare programs than it had been 30 years before. To be sure, businessmen had always donated their time and money to charitable endeavors; but businessmen in the 1960's were interested in social problems as never before. [45] Frederick R. Kappel, board chairman of American Telephone and Telegraph Company, reminded businessmen that the "social responsibilities of business are increasing." The civil rights movement and the anguish of summer riots in major cities were pointed reminders that poverty and hopelessness were concentrated among Negroes. Job discrimination and lack of training had contributed to the racial crisis. Businessmen drew the obvious conclusion that they must grapple with these problems if the civil disorder and riots were not to shake the very foundations of the society. Participation in antipoverty programs, creation of special job and training programs, and membership in the Urban Coalition formed in 1967—all these were manifestations of business concern over the social issues of race and poverty.

Hard economic facts also argued for business participation in the poverty program at the inception of OEO. Prior to the Vietnam escalation of summer 1965, many businessmen were concerned about actual or anticipated reductions in federal defense and space spending. The problem of adjusting from "guns to butter" weighed especially heavily upon the large defense contractors who had extensive resources tied up in government contracting activities and who could not easily adjust these to a consumer market. One solution would be to diversify some manufacturing to services—the growth industries of the future.

And among the service industries, education and training offered the most promising opportunities. Such a shift would not be as far-fetched as it sounded because management believed that many of the "systems" concepts developed in the production of hardware could also be applied to human resources. Contracts from OEO for specialized educational tasks, let on a cost-plus basis, would offer a risk-free opportunity for business to "get in on the ground floor," experiment with new techniques, and develop the expertise needed to exploit this market.[46] Secondary motivations for business involvement no doubt included the desire to make a useful contribution and the realization that business must respond if its own long-term needs for skilled manpower were to be met.

The Job Corps offered a particularly useful vehicle for this business involvement. It was John Rubel, Vice President of Litton Industries, who first suggested to Shriver that private industries might run the Job Corps training centers. As a direct result, Title I was written to authorize OEO's Director to contract with "any federal, state, or local agency or *private organization* for the establishment and operation of rural or urban Job Corps centers" (Section 103[a]).[Italics added.] The largest share of funds for urban Job Corps centers went to private industries. Contracts were awarded to such firms as the Burroughs Corporation, General Electric, Ford-Philco Corporation, International Telephone and Telegraph, International Business Machines, Litton Industries, and Packard-Bell Electronics Corporation. Many other firms received or applied for contracts.

The business-government partnership may well turn out to be profitable for all concerned. To be sure, the profits cannot be measured in monetary terms. "Most of the companies aren't in this just for money," explained Milton Fogelman, OEO's contract negotiator. "This is not a staggeringly profitable business," agreed Robert Chasen, President of Federal Electric Corporation, an IT&T subsidiary which had the contract for the Kilmer Job Corps Center. But to have the federal government underwrite a firm's experimentation in a promising field (and on a cost-plus-fixed-fee basis) is an attractive proposition.

Not quite all of OEO's activities were enthusiastically received by the business community. Traditional business opposition to governmental paternalism continued to express itself from time to time. Other complaints were more specific. Some businessmen, for example, complained that CAA's were sponsoring consumer education programs which adversely affected local retail merchants. In some cases, it was charged, "consumer advisors" directed consumers into or away from specific stores, propagated their own judgments as to what constituted "deceptive" packaging, and instigated such "massive mobilization" of the poor as boycotts or buyer's strikes.[47] It is entirely possible that local poverty workers sometimes attempted to give consumer advice when in fact they possessed little information beyond personal prejudices against local businesses. On the other hand, the impoverished have long been the victims not only of their own ignorance of buying practices, but also of the manipulations of irresponsible businessmen. The poor desperately need guidance; and complaints over the type of advice they have so far received only emphasize how little attention our consumer-oriented society has actually given to consumption practices.

The labor movement, as one of its recent publications declared, "has been enlisted in the war on poverty from the day the first union was organized."[48] Organized labor was an early supporter of the Economic Opportunity Act, and has continued to give strong political support to OEO. In February 1967, the AFL-CIO Executive Council termed the Act "a vital part of the over-all effort to break the poverty cycle," and repudiated "attacks . . . aimed at crippling or destroying the entire program."[49] In early 1965, AFL-CIO President George Meany named Miles C. Stanley, West Virginia AFL-CIO president, as a special aide to coordinate labor participation in antipoverty programs. And Walter Reuther's United Auto Workers gave consistently strong support to the programs—including, in 1965, a $1 million grant to create a public organization called the Citizens Crusade Against Poverty (CCAP).

At the local level, labor unions are frequent participants in CAA programs. In fact, CAP guidelines stress that local union officers—along with representatives of other interests—should be consulted in drawing up the community action plan. In some cases unions have become contractors for antipoverty programs: an engineers' union in Tennessee launched a Job Corps training program, for example; and a number of central labor councils have participated in NYC programs.[50] To serve as a link between organized labor and OEO, there is a National Labor Advisory Council, which was described by its OEO staff man as "a channel of communication that has provided some program results."

Labor's support has not been unequivocal, however. Some unions feared that jobs for nonunion workers might come at the expense of union members—a fear which led to some early suspicions about the work of the Shriver task force and was sustained by demands of some CAA's that the poor be hired to rehabilitate slum areas. Nor were all unions equally active participants in local antipoverty programs. Shriver candidly told a national labor convention in December 1965 that "despite the leadership and the vision demonstrated by our own leaders, there has been a dragging of the feet at the local level." Reuther has been even more pointed and has laid some of the blame on AFL-CIO leadership: in 1966 he charged that the AFL-CIO policy on social welfare and antipoverty questions demonstrated "insufficient commitment" and "a sense of complacency and adherence to the *status quo.*"[51]

OEO and the Civil Rights Movement

Although the majority of poor people in the United States are white, the battle against poverty has become an adjunct to the battle for Negro equality. The ties are no less strong because those who drafted the Economic Opportunity Act of 1964 were unaware that they were drafting a civil rights law. In a thousand different ways, black citizens have become the special objects and beneficiaries of antipoverty programs. While not confined to Negroes, economic deprivation is especially prevalent among this segment of our population and is related to educational inequalities, job discrimination, and social and political injustices. Moreover, the first phase of the modern civil rights struggle—the fight for political and social rights—gave the Negro (especially in urban areas) an organizational base which was lacking among whites who were poor. For these and other reasons, Negroes received from the antipoverty programs greater benefits than their proportion of the poor population would have indicated. Indeed, it was possible to view the early OEO as a potential institutional base for the second phase of the civil rights movement: the achievement of more effective economic participation in our society.

In reality, however, OEO found itself caught between the civil rights militants and the white "establishment." At first, the views of civil rights militants were effectively represented by militants within the OEO organization. As time went on, it became apparent that OEO would have to settle for something short of the militant objectives; and within a year or so, many militants left OEO. The antipoverty programs came under increasing criticism from civil rights activists. Thus, civil rights tensions were intimately tied to the political tensions OEO was experiencing with city halls and the social welfare establishment. As an NAACP official expressed the problem in mid-1965:

> We must rescue the anti-poverty program from the social work profession and from the politicians who want merely a sterile and ineffective program that will mean little or nothing for the Negro community . . . .

> We must shed the illusion that this is a war on poverty—it is merely a beebee shot against it. A real war on poverty would require fundamental alterations in our national economy and the mobilization of a significant portion of the national income for this purpose.[52]

Such sentiments were shared by many militant activists, white and black, inside OEO and out. Nonetheless, most Negro organizations continued to play an active role in antipoverty programs. The National Urban League, for example, worked to recruit Job Corps enrollees, operated some NYC projects, and served as a delegate agency for CAA projects.

In local communities, the ferment of the civil rights movement sometimes generated problems for OEO's relations with other outside interests. For instance, a minor controversy arose when it was discovered that a multi-million dollar HARYOU-Act program was subsidizing a theater program known as the "Black Arts Theatre"—which was using some of the funds to stage some anti-white plays by Negro dramatist LeRoi Jones. The plays were offensive to many citizens, and Shriver himself referred to them as "vicious racism." However, even such a controversial activity may have had some redeeming value. As OEO Deputy Director of Public Affairs James Kelleher remarked, "We'd rather see these kids fussing on the stage than on the streets."[53]

A similar flurry of criticism arose in the summer of 1967 when it was discovered that one of the items proposed in the summer package of a delegate agency of the Nashville, Tennessee, CAA called for a "Liberation School."[54] In this case, OEO ordered the funds which were to be allocated for that part of the proposal to be withdrawn.

Potentially more explosive was the National Center for Community Action Education, Inc., a group created to combine private and foundation funds with federal grants for a major assault on illiteracy. James Farmer, National Director of the Congress of Racial Equality (CORE), resigned his position late in 1965 to take over the new organization. Farmer's presence suggested that the group would be concerned not only with adult basic education—its ostensible objective—but with political mobilization of the poor. The National Center, endorsed by every major civil rights group, soon applied for a grant of $860,000 from OEO to launch a pilot adult education program. OEO project reviewers and outside experts agreed that the program—which would have trained poor persons to teach others—was "an unconventional but promising venture."[55]

Farmer's program was never funded because political pressures developed against it. A number of Congressmen reportedly feared the political implications of a mass literacy drive, and they were no doubt backed up by local politicians. The crucial opponent of the program, however, was Adam Clayton Powell, then chairman of the House Education and Labor Committee. Though Powell never explained his position (a restraint unusual for Powell), OEO acquiesced to the pressures and killed the proposal in mid-1966, explaining only that "this proposal just hasn't made it up to this point."[56] The explanation lacked candor, since the proposal (submitted in August 1965) had apparently passed all OEO's reviewers and was so close to funding in late 1965 that news was leaked on the plan's funding. Farmer, who had resigned his CORE job on the assumption that funding was imminent, charged OEO with "a colossal betrayal" and sent Shriver a telegram which stated:

> Your failure to communicate with me in any way whatsoever is far more than a personal affront; it is another broken promise to millions of Americans who are more and more outside the main stream of American life . . . . We can wait no longer for OEO to

back a meaningful assault on this vital aspect of poverty.[57]

Though OEO officially denied that political pressures had killed the project, some officials informally confirmed the fact.

In other ways OEO became inevitably involved in the ferment of the civil rights movement. In most cases, OEO had the courage of its convictions in insisting that Negroes be included in its programs. The controversies over "maximum feasible participation," for example, often had racial overtones. Here OEO tended to be flexible, but without losing sight of its directions: full participation by Negro citizens in policy evolution and implementation.

OEO has taken to civil rights instinctively, but it is hard to say whether it recognizes fully the centrality of civil rights to its task. If our repeated observations are on the mark, OEO will ultimately be evaluated more for its role in the political mobilization of disadvantaged citizens than for the actual number of dollars it puts into their pocketbooks. Civil rights groups have provided direction and purpose for OEO's tasks, and in many cases they have supplied the bulk of the skilled leadership. Whether OEO will be successful in meeting the demands of Negro groups is open to question and depends on a variety of factors, not the least of which are the resources available to the agency and the future role of local governments. And whether the poverty program can at the same time mobilize the non-Negroes among the poor depends on the insight and perspective of both OEO and the Negro action groups.

The Care and Cultivation of Clienteles

From the inception of the antipoverty programs, it was clearly understood that one of their major objectives was to mobilize private as well as public welfare activities. This goal emerged from the legislative history, from the wording of the Act itself, and from President Johnson's various messages on poverty. Thus OEO has paid particular attention to its "external affairs." Such activity is not entirely unique within the federal government. The State Department has long had a program to involve nongovernmental organizations in understanding and supporting the nation's foreign policy. Additionally, many agencies employ advisory councils or committees which are composed of representatives of groups served by the agencies' programs.

The bulk of OEO's formal relationships with nongovernmental organizations is handled by its Office of National Councils and Organizations (ONCO), headed during the first three years by Hyman Bookbinder. (From a recently popular television program, Bookbinder quickly earned the title of "The Man from ONCO.") Not an operating office, ONCO provides such service functions as information, liaison, and coordination with private groups. In addition, Bookbinder—a vigorous and accomplished speaker—served as one of OEO's most prolific spokesmen, spreading the OEO gospel with inimitable fervor and replying to countless criticisms of the agency.

ONCO also serves as secretariat for most of the advisory councils established by OEO. The first of these, the National Advisory Council on Economic Opportunity, is composed of private individuals appointed by the President. For two years ONCO coordinated the group's activities, but a 1966 amendment made the group independent of OEO. The new chairman of the group (Shriver had served in this capacity until 1966) was Morris L. Liebman, a Chicago lawyer. The revamped Council, all but three of whose members were new to the group, was strongly representative of politicians, southerners (and Texans), and friends of the President. In the newly-constituted group there was but one Negro, one economist, and one woman. In addition, the President authorized a small staff of investigators, presumably to help the Council monitor OEO's activities. When asked for his reaction to this development, Shriver replied: "It doesn't bother me a bit. In fact, I welcome it. The more people who take a hard look at this program, the better off we are going to be."[58] So far, the group has received minimal publicity and apparently has given OEO no cause for worry.

In addition, OEO's Director is empowered to create such advisory groups as he deems necessary (Section 602[c]). By late 1967, Shriver had created five such groups. The first, chronologically, were the Business and Labor Advisory Councils—both served by ONCO. A Public Officials Advisory Council, composed of 26 local governmental representatives, was created in the fall of 1965 as part of OEO's efforts to improve its contacts with local and state officials. Originally linked with

ONCO, this group was later transferred to OEO's Office of Governmental Relations. In early 1966, a 28-member Community Representative Advisory Council was created. The title was a euphemism for a "council of the poor," since the membership was composed of what one OEO official termed "articulate, independent, local CAA people who are also recognized as representatives of the poor." Two-thirds of the members were themselves poor, and about the same proportion were Negro. Frankly experimental, this group represented an effort by OEO to obtain direct responses from the representatives of the poor.[59] Though the group's role was strictly as sounding-board for OEO policies, officials conceded that many thoughtful critiques originated there. The establishment of a national council representing the poor received much public attention, but little was heard from the group during the following years. Finally, late in 1967, a Women's Advisory Council was created. The latter two groups are both served by ONCO.

ONCO also deals, formally or otherwise, with many other groups, including local government representatives, church groups, and welfare organizations. Many established interest groups—ranging from the AFL-CIO and the National Council of Churches to the U.S. Chamber of Commerce and the American Bankers Association—have created special committees or task forces on poverty. It is ONCO's function to provide liaison between OEO and these private sector organizations.

Footnotes

[36] U.S. Congress, House Committee on Education and Labor, *Economic Opportunity Act,* Report on H.R. 10440, Report 1458, 88th Cong., 2nd Sess., (Washington: Government Printing Office, 1964), p. 11.

[37] *Congressional Record* (Daily Edition), August 6, 1964, pp. 17674-76.

[38] Section 124(a)(3). This identical provision also appears in the Higher Education Act of 1965 (P.L. 89-329), Section 441 (a)(2)(B).

[39] The suit was filed by Protestants and Other Americans United for Separation of Church and State (POAU). *The New York Times,* August 2, 1965.

[40] *Poverty,* a statement by the Interreligious Committee Against Poverty (Washington, 1967), p. 3.

56

4 1 Austin C. Wehrwein, "Shriver Calls on Social Workers to Help Antipoverty Campaign," *The New York Times,* December 3, 1965.

4 2 Address to the American Public Welfare Association, Chicago, Illinois, December 2, 1965.

4 3 Task Force on Economic Growth and Opportunity, Chamber of Commerce of the United States, *The Concept of Poverty; Poverty: The Sick, Disabled and Aged;* and *The Disadvantaged Poor* (Washington: The Chamber, 1965 and 1966).

4 4 Dennis Duggan, "Blue Chips Sign Up in War on Poverty," *New York Herald Tribune,* February 28, 1965.

4 5 Stephen Kurzman, "Private Enterprise Participation in the Antipoverty Program," see Footnote 10, Vol.I, pp. 89-148; and William C. Selover, "The Other War on Poverty: Stepping into Aid-to-Poor Gaps," *The Christian Science Monitor,* December 28, 1966.

4 6 John McHale, "Big Business Enlists for the War on Poverty," *Trans-Action,* May-June 1965, pp. 3-9.

4 7 Paul Hencke, "Is War on Poverty Becoming War on Business?" *Nation's Business,* March 1966, p. 40 ff.

4 8 AFL-CIO, *Labor's Role in the War on Poverty* (Washington: AFL-CIO, 1965), p. 1.

4 ° "The War on Poverty," statement of the AFL-CIO Executive Council, Bal Harbour, Florida, February 1967.

5 0 William C. Selover, "Labor Leaders Find Active Role in Fight Against Poverty," *The Christian Science Monitor,* January 5, 1967.

5 1 *Ibid.*

5 2 Quoted in Donald Pfarrer, "NAACP Polled Poverty War is More 'White Paternalism'," *The Washington Evening Star,* June 29, 1965.

5 3 *Baltimore Sun,* December 1, 1965.

5 4 OEO Press Release 67-203, August 3, 1967, and Stuart Auerbach, "Hate School Got U.S. Aid, Police Say," *The Washington Post,* August 4, 1967.

5 5 Editorial, "Farmer, Powell and the OEO," *The New York Times,* July 9, 1965.

[56] Accounts of the history of the proposal are found in: Joseph Loftus, "Doomed Literacy Drive," *The New York Times,* July 6, 1966; and Ernest A. Ostro, "Suddenly, A Project to Teach Illiterates Was Dead," *The Washington Evening Star*, August 23, 1966.

[57] Gerald Grant, "OEO Denies Politics Stalled Farmer Feud," *The Washington Post,* July 5, 1966.

[58] Joseph Loftus, "Council to Guide Poverty Agency," *The New York Times,* March 23, 1967.

[59] Robert Walters, "Poor Get Top Poverty Advisory Role," *The Washington Evening Star,* January 23, 1966.

FINANCIAL TROUBLES

Of all OEO travails, those associated with funding were the most serious impediment to efficient and smooth operations. That there was not enough money to wage "an unconditional war on poverty" needs no repetition; but the way Congress handled the annual OEO appropriations bears particular emphasis. The antipoverty warriors were treated in the manner to which the poor, whom they represented, have always been accustomed. The annual handout was given grudgingly, with all manner of strings attached and with delays as long as possible. Even within the usual constraints of annual budgeting, Congress seemed to do its utmost to prevent orderly planning and administration of EOA efforts.

Congress must undertake two separate steps before a federal agency can receive spending money. The first step is authorization of an activity or program, and the second step is appropriation of funds to implement the enabling legislation. The first step involves also the authorization of funds, but this need not be specific; the enabling legislation need authorize only "whatever appropriations are deemed necessary" to carry out the given piece of legislation.

In the case of the Economic Opportunity Act, Congress determined each of the first three years to limit the authorization of expenditures to only one year, requiring an annual review of the enabling legislation before funds could be appropriated. In 1967, Congress authorized expenditures of funds for two years.

During each of the first three years of EOA, Congress delayed not only the appropriations of the agency, but also the enabling legislation. In 1967, nearly half of the fiscal year 1968 had passed before Congress approved the EOA enabling legislation and appropriations. Since a federal agency is prohibited from spending unappropriated funds beginning with each fiscal year (starting on July first), Congress normally passes a "continuing resolution" permitting each agency whose appropriations have not been approved to continue operations at the same level of expenditure as during the previous year. In the case of long-established agencies with continuing and stable programs, such delays may not be too damaging. However, this did not apply to the EOA, whose programs changed from year to year. These alterations thus required that OEO juggle its fund allocations in midstream, retrenching on-going programs and expanding new ones, to adjust to the ever-changing mandates of Congress—which normally did not provide adequate funds to meet the requirements of new programs.

OEO sometimes compounded its difficulties. For example, in response to pressures to expand assistance to rural areas, it funded 135 CAA's during fiscal 1967 giving them initial grants for program development. "What that really means," Shriver explained to a Senate Appropriations Subcommittee pleading for additional funds, "we gave them enough money to get set up to go into business . . . . We have to have more money to finance their operations."[60] OEO can hardly be faulted for generating pressure to get some additional funds, but the point is that effective planning was precluded. Commenting on this problem, Paul N. Ylvisaker, Director of Community Affairs for New Jersey, a veteran antipoverty warrior and one of the most sophisticated men in the business, stated:

> Even more important than the amounts of money to be made available, is the more secure commitment of funds over a longer period of time, and I would like to emphasize this: No industry I know of would venture the development of a new product on a sudden-death basis and with uncertain financing. Yet this is what the poverty program has had to do—attempting fundamental reforms and incredibly complex innovations on short-time budgets subject to change without notice.[61]

OEO had precious little money to fight its "war." Fiscally, 1964 was a propitious time for launching the war; the economy was expanding (which it continued to do during the following three years), and the efficient federal revenue system assured that the government would get its share of the growing national product. The preoccupation of economists in those days was the comforting one (considering later developments) that federal tax collections would create a fiscal drag slowing down economic growth. Two major alternatives were available—to cut taxes or expand federal expenditures. Policy shapers found the first alternative more to their liking, and tax cuts were adopted in 1964 and again in the following year. Future expansion of expenditures was not excluded, however, and antipoverty planners hoped to get a good share of the "automatic" increases in federal revenue.

When the war on poverty was launched in 1964 with only modest resources, it was assumed that the programs would be rapidly expanded and new ones added as the situation required. The funds were there, but they never materialized. And initially, at least, it was not because the nation had to make a choice between "guns and butter"—the escalation of the war in Vietnam was still in the future. Nonetheless, when the President presented in 1965 his budget for the following year, he requested $1.5 billion for OEO. Superficially, this appeared to support the commitment to wage the domestic war, since Congress had appropriated about half of that amount for the initial year of OEO. The apparent increase was misleading, however, since the $800 million appropriated for fiscal 1965 was considered by OEO officials and other supporters of the antipoverty effort to be adequate only for launching and certainly not for fighting the "war." It is known that before the budgetary request of $1.5 billion for fiscal 1966 was made public, several of Shriver's closest advisors urged him to demand more funds for OEO and to offer his resignation if the demands were not approved. Of course, the President had other welfare items on his agenda—Medicare and federal aid to education, to mention the most significant bills. The confrontation between the President and Shriver apparently never took place, and by the time the next budget was presented to Congress, the nation was facing two wars. The war on poverty was not escalated but continued at an even pace; the increases were adequate to cover average boosts in wages and salaries with little left for expansion.

While Congress is usually blamed for blocking expansion of EOA programs, the President must share the responsibility. The best opportunity to expand EOA programs existed in 1965, but the President did not take advantage of it. It is generally conceded that the 89th Congress (1965-1966) was the most liberal in more than a generation. In 1965, Congress authorized more funds for OEO than the President requested but appropriated the full amount the President recommended. The next two years, Congress trimmed the amount the President recommended. Even OEO finally despaired of expanding its programs. In the fall of 1965, when the agency submitted its budget for the following year, starting July 1, 1966, OEO asked for $3.4 billion, but the Administration cut the request by nearly one-half and requested of Congress only $1.75 billion.[62] A year later, OEO lowered its sights and requested $900 million less than it did in 1965, but indicated that it would settle for a "low option" of $1.85 billion, almost as much as Congress appropriated.[63]

Had EOA programs been given the opportunity to expand in 1965, it is not likely that Congress would have cut existing programs during the subsequent two years. It is easier to prevent expansion of programs than to retrench on-going efforts. Reduction of the OEO budget would have meant loss of jobs in communities and elimination of services. Few Congressmen would take such a step lightly. The President's annual recommended budget, authorization, and actual appropriation to OEO between 1964 and 1967 is presented in Table 4.

Table 4
OEO Budget: Presidential Request, Congressional Authorization and Appropriation.
Fiscal 1965-1968

Fiscal Year	President's Request (Millions)	Authorization (Millions)	Appropriation (Millions)
1965	$ 947.5	$ 947.5	$ 800.0*
1966	1,500.0	1,785.0	1,500.0
1967	1,750.0	1,750.0	1,687.5
1968	2,060.0	1,980.0	1,773.0

*Covered only part of fiscal year since appropriation was voted after first quarter of year had elapsed.

Source: Office of Economic Opportunity.

While appropriations rose only slightly, Congress persisted in adding to OEO's responsibilities and earmarking specific amounts for the new activities. Since appropriations did not provide sufficient additional funds to cover the new activities, OEO was forced to reallocate funds among EOA programs. This annual robbing-Peter-to-pay-Paul exercise further delayed the allocation of funds to specific programs. OEO's difficulties were compounded by the fact that the annual appropriation was made in a lump sum, and the agency was not free to distribute the funds due to constraints imposed in the authorizing legislation which, beginning with fiscal 1966, specified the amounts to be allocated to each program. However, the authorized funds exceeded the actual appropriations each year. To distribute the available funds among the several claimants, protracted negotiations were required. These were complicated by the fact that the administration of some programs was delegated to agencies outside OEO. By the time a program administrator knew the exact amount that would be allocated to his activity, half of the fiscal year or more had passed. As a result, there was an annual scramble at the end of the fiscal year to obligate available funds lest they expire at the end of the year. In 1966 and 1967, nearly 40 percent of the total annual appropriations were obligated during the last two months of the year; and in 1967, more than a fourth of the total appropriation was obligated during the final month of the fiscal year. Despite the annual eleventh-hour rush, program administrators did lose part of their funds. During the first two years OEO lost a total of $100 million, nearly four percent of the appropriated funds. In the third year the unobligated funds diminished to a trickle and amounted to .4 percent of total appropriations.

There may be a considerable wait from the time the funds are obligated until they are expended. It takes time to spend money. Only two-thirds of the nearly $4 billion that Congress appropriated during the first three years of the program was expended by the end of that period (Table 5). As the various programs developed and attracted their clienteles, the demand expanded. Not only did total expenditures rise each year in absolute terms, but the proportion of expenditures to available funds also continued to mount. During the fourth year of OEO, expenditures could actually exceed the appropriations for that year, drawing from the unexpended funds during the preceding

Table 5

OEO Allocations, Obligations and Expenditures
By Program, Fiscal Years, 1965-1967

Program	Title EOA	Allocations (Millions)	Obligations (Millions)	Expenditures Millions	Expenditures Percentage of Allocated Funds
Total		3968.7	3872.7	2756.6	69
Job Corps	IA	704.0	712.2	651.6	93
NYC	IB	776.5	766.2	559.7	72
Adult Work	IB	84.9	84.4	3.4	4
CAP	II	1745.1	1670.3	1049.7	60
Rural Loans	IIIA	84.7	78.4	78.4	93
Migrant Workers	IIIB	74.0	73.5	45.1	61
Work Experience and Training	V	324.0	318.6	217.3	67
VISTA	VIII	45.2	45.3	39.1	86
Administration		33.5	31.2	24.6	73
Adult Literacy*		40.0	36.7	31.8	80
Work-Study*		56.8·	55.9	55.9	98

*Transferred to Health, Education, and Welfare.

Source: Office of Economic Opportunity.

years. Should that occur, there would be increased pressures upon Congress to increase OEO's appropriations as more people participate in the programs.

There was wide variation in the extent to which OEO programs managed to expend their available funds. The rural loan program was the most efficient spender, having nothing unexpended out of the $78 million obligated under the program. The Job Corps had a slow start, but during the third year, it lived above its current means and used up most of the unexpended funds left during the preceding years. The Job Corps was forced to retrench during fiscal 1968 when Congress failed to appropriate adequate funds for the program to continue expenditures at the level of the preceding years. Of the major programs, CAP was the most laggard spender, accounting by the end of fiscal 1967 for three-fifths of OEO's total unexpended funds.

Footnotes

[60] U.S. Congress, Senate Committee on Appropriations, *Supplemental Appropriations for Fiscal Year 1968,* 90th Cong., 1st Sess., (Washington: Government Printing Office, 1968), p. 3.

[61] See Footnote 15, Part 1, p. 134.

[62] U.S. Congress, House Appropriations Committee, Hearings, *Supplemental Appropriation Bill, 1967,* 89th Cong., 2nd Sess., (Washington: Government Printing Office, 1966), p. 40.

[63] U.S. Congress, House Appropriations Committee, Hearings, *Supplemental Appropriation Bill, 1968,* 90th Cong., 1st Sess., (Washington: Government Printing Office, 1967), p. 141.

PUBLIC AND CONGRESSIONAL RELATIONS

Since the appointment of the Shriver task force in early 1964, the nation's war on poverty has remained in the public eye. The nation's press, which had ignored the trial balloons sent forth by the Administration in mid-1963, responded enthusiastically in 1964 to the Economic Opportunity Act. This interest remained only slightly abated after the first three years of OEO. Writing in 1966, two knowledgeable journalists observed that "the war on poverty has ranked second only to the related area of civil rights as a continuing domestic news story."[64] From 15 to 20 Washington newmen include OEO in their regular "beat"—not to mention the countless local reporters who write about the antipoverty programs from time to time. Although such attention is not always desirable, it has signaled the elevation of poverty to the status of a major public issue for the first time since the New Deal. Few federal agencies have been more exposed to the mass media than OEO.

OEO began its work in a flurry of favorable publicity. President Johnson's "unconditional war on poverty" caught the fancy of the press and public; and selection of Shriver as "the field general" of the war added luster to the effort. Shriver was able to bring across the poverty message effectively. For the field general and his "poverty warriors" (as they came to be called), OEO's first year must have been a heady experience.

OEO has been expertly organized to capitalize on its relation with the communications media. Its information program is specifically authorized in the Economic Opportunity Act, which empowers OEO's Director to distribute "data and information, in such form as he shall deem appropriate, to public agencies, private organizations and the general public." [65] The agency has taken this injunction to heart. Its Office of Public Affairs, which late in

1967 employed 52 people, was headed by Herbert J. Kramer, formerly in charge of public relations and advertising for a large insurance company. "We're organized in a sense like an in-house advertising agency," Kramer stated. "It's patterned after my own experience in a 72-man operation in a multi-product organization." [66] He explained that his office follows both "vertical" and "horizontal" tables of organization: vertically, staff members specialize in major OEO programs (which lack their own public information staffs); horizontally, staff members specialize in various media techniques.

The Office performs a full range of publicity and public relations functions. Standard news releases, weekly progress bulletins, and summaries of press comments are prepared routinely. In addition, the Office conducts seminars for journalists, draws up presentations of OEO activities, answers criticisms of the agency, and is generally available to the press (ten phone lines are open during office hours). Finally, there are more esoteric ventures—a comic book on OEO was commissioned from cartoonist Al Capp and half a million copies were printed, and VISTA training films (not shown to the general public) won Academy Award nominations in 1967 and 1968. Some of OEO's publicity gambits have raised eyebrows; at one point, OEO persuaded a network rock-n-roll television personality to appeal to disadvantaged teenagers to participate in OEO programs. Though the idea was innovative and sensible, a storm of editorial and Congressional criticism ensued—presumably because these representatives of middle-class values could not see the connection between disadvantaged youth and rock-n-roll.

The very success of OEO's early publicity was unfortunate, if only because the agency could not hope to live up to the fanfares. Lacking reliable data or experience, OEO officials sometimes created projections of success which they later conceded were "visionary" or "unrealistic." Until the launching of Operation Head Start in the summer of 1965, OEO had no real programs operating in the field—only grants, which were invariably accompanied by announcements and elaborate signing ceremonies. Even after the successful conclusion of the first summer's Head Start program, no hard figures existed to lend substance to OEO's press claims. In this vacuum, OEO officials succumbed to the "numbers game," making unrealistic promises and projections. The agency's first Congressional presentation, for example, contained figures which were (in the words of one official) "generated out of whole cloth."

Even after OEO's programs had begun to generate real accomplishments and frustrations, public reporting by the agency continued to leave much to be desired. First, there existed a credibility gap in some of the statistics. Expenditures per enrollee in the Job Corps, for example, were the subject of conflicting reports with several revisions of the figures. Second, public statements by OEO officials often utilized such imprecise words as "reached," "affected," or "served," when describing the scope or impact of programs. These statements typically failed to specify the ways in which the programs "affected" poor people: "affected" could mean anything from giving a word of encouragement to providing a job or training experience. Third, OEO naturally sought to interpret its statistics in the most favorable light. OEO's propensity to exaggerate success claims is legion and needs no repetition here.

In a larger sense, OEO's public information activities—aided and abetted, it must be stressed, by the news media—had the effect of raising expectations that could never be fulfilled. As an example, Shriver in 1966 exhorted Congress to eliminate poverty by 1976—the 200th anniversary of the Declaration of Independence. Few would quarrel with such a goal. However, Shriver neglected to tell Congress that achievement of this goal would require additional expenditures of at least $20 billion annually in aid of the poor. It is hard to see what benefit such pronouncements served as long as they were unaccompanied by an indication of their costs, their prospects for implementation, and their realistic chances of success. Indeed, unfulfilled promises of this sort have given added ammunition to foes of the poverty programs; and what is more important, they have created cruel disappointment among those who hoped to benefit.

Only with difficulty has OEO outgrown its youthful enthusiasm. The agency's expansive handling of the press during the first year and a half was perhaps to be expected, given the high-minded enthusiasm of the poverty efforts, the journalistic backgrounds of a number of OEO officials, and the style of OEO's Director. In 1966, however, Kramer's office began to counteract the earlier press-agentry and exercise more caution. First, the big, circus-like press conferences were abandoned. Second, the elaborate ceremonies for signing each contract were eliminated.

All press releases on local grants and programs are handled by OEO's regional offices. Third, few new programs have been launched since the early days, a fact which has decreased the opportunities for making extravagant claims. Finally, OEO initiated a policy of making evaluation reports available to outsiders.

The softening of OEO's early "hard sell" has not deterred the critics who charge that OEO spends an inordinate amount of resources on public information. [67] On the other hand, these same critics are in part responsible for OEO's constant need for cultivation of its public image. For example, the appendix of the *Congressional Record* is full of stories on OEO's shortcomings, both large and small, inserted by hostile Congressmen. Moreover, it must be recognized that antipoverty programs are by nature scandal-prone. There are two reasons for this. First, the participants in poverty programs are not solid, middle-class citizens; they are people who are unemployed, or uneducated, or bitter, often high risks because of a prison record. If—as might occur—they get into trouble while enrolled in an OEO program, their transgressions are easy targets for hostile politicians or journalists of the "man-bites-dog" approach to newsgathering. Second, many of those in charge of local OEO programs were well-meaning but inexperienced. For example, a worker in Texas decided to purchase old gunsights to use as microscopes for a training project; the resultant "scandal," which falsely implied that he was buying guns to arm Negro trainees, had to be dealt with.

OEO's original philosophy was that criticism should be answered swiftly. "We owe this to the poor," Kramer explained. "We've got to come back fast." While early rebuttals might have served to quash the charges, there were at least two disadvantages to this strategy. First, carefully documented responses to charges often require time to prepare. Second, OEO's seeming sensitivity to criticism may have given the critics' charges more attention than they really deserved.

OEO began to show greater restraint as time wore on—and particularly after Bertrand M. Harding became Deputy Director, and later head of the agency. OEO officials maintained in early 1968 that they insisted on documentation before releasing rebuttals. As one of them remarked: "The simple wise crack response went out long ago."

In defending itself, OEO sometimes went far beyond clarification of factual matters. Direct attacks upon critics were sometimes indulged in, as when OEO press releases referred to a statement of Representative William Ayres (ranking Republican on the House Education and Labor Committee) as "typical misrepresentation for political purposes"; and to House Minority Leader Gerald Ford as "the only Ford that acts like an Edsel when he'd like to be a Mustang." [68]

Perhaps the most extreme use of this technique occurred in mid-1966, when OEO decided to take on the Republican National Committee. The object of OEO's ire was a Republican report which had urged drastic revisions of antipoverty programs, including spin-off of several key programs to other federal and local agencies. These reforms, the report explained, were based on "the Republican approach to *assist* the poor and disadvantaged in their climb up the economic and social ladder; not to *drag* them up forcibly by a green rope of dollar bills." [69] OEO lost no time in replying. Its press release, dated the very same day as the GOP press release, was nothing more than a string of superficial rebuttals of the Republican arguments. Particularly impolitic were partisan remarks like the following:

> Using the familiar techniques of the oft-repeated inaccuracy and distortion, paying no heed to facts, the Republicans are engaged in a carefully-planned attempt to destroy public confidence in [OEO] ....
> [OEO] welcomes responsible review of the antipoverty program but it resents the hit-and-run guerilla warfare of Republican poverty memos and party pronouncements .... Those hurt most by Republican cynicism and ill-founded criticism of the War on Poverty are the poor themselves. The Republican party will conveniently forget them when election day is over. [70]

If anything, OEO's response served to give the Republican charges more readership than that usually accorded the pronouncements of national party committees. And it gave Republicans further cause for resentment against OEO. A few days later, House Minority Leader Ford stated that the agency had concentrated on publicity while neglecting the poor, and demanded an end to "the use of public funds for a partisan attack upon the Republican party by a government agency." [71]

This incident was perhaps OEO's most controversial foray into the political use of the press release. But it was by no means unique. One can sympathize with the natural frustration of dedicated public officials under attack; but greater tactical restraint in such cases would certainly have been advisable. As it was, Republican spokesmen continued their attacks upon the OEO publicity mills.

During the House hearings on OEO the following year, Charles Goodell (R-N.Y.) referred to some articles in which Shriver was quoted as accusing Republicans of being throat slitters and doing professional hatchet jobs. Chiding Shriver, he went on to say, "Glib terms like 'throat slitting,' 'professional hatchet job' . . . don't advance the cause of good legislation at all." [72]

Another problem faced by OEO's Office of Public Affairs was that of controlling adverse stories emanating from within the agency itself. Especially in its first years, OEO possessed a large number of restless and articulate staff members who had many contacts within the press corps. Moreover, these staff people understood how to use the press. Thus, when they ended up on the losing side of an issue or factional dispute within the agency, they had a habit of airing their grievances publicly. This gave the impression, perhaps somewhat exaggerated (though not greatly so), that OEO had a hotbed of factionalism and dissatisfaction. Under Kramer's direction, the Public Affairs Office endeavored to centralize OEO's press relations, suggesting that OEO officials advise Public Affairs of their conversations with newsmen. The suggestion was apparently no more than that, but some OEO officials interpreted it as an order and conveyed this interpretation to reporters. Protests from reporters produced a "clarifying" memo (dated June 8, 1966) reaffirming an "open door" policy.

OEO's Public Affairs Office has perhaps the most demanding public information assignment in Washington. Poverty programs are newsworthy but vulnerable to unfavorable publicity. Not only political opponents of the program, but well-meaning reporters whose concept of significant news extends no further than scandal hunting, are untiring in their search for flaws in the implementation of antipoverty programs. And given the inherent design of the programs and the character of their clienteles, OEO is often the victim of a bad press. A mature response to this problem would probably acknowledge it as unavoidable and try to help the media place their stories in proper perspective. But the "mature" response is not an easy one, either psychologically or politically, for it presupposes a "mature" public which is willing to accept "scandals" as the inevitable price of achieving difficult objectives. It is little wonder, then, that OEO officials sometimes appeared over-sensitive to criticism or exposure in the nation's press.

A corollary of OEO's media exposure, and a partial cause of it, is the political exposure of the antipoverty efforts. The first fact that bears emphasis is the relatively low level of political participation on the part of disadvantaged people in the United States. Other things being equal, poor people are less likely to vote, to take part in other political activities, or even to have much information about politics. If the poor do not participate, they are not a promising object of the politicians' attentions. As John Kenneth Galbraith has written,"Any politician who speaks for the poor is speaking for a small and also an inarticulate minority."[73]

At the outset at least, therefore, OEO's clientele had only limited political resources with which to defend their claims. One segment of this clientele—the civil rights movement—did possess impressive organization and influence, and indeed was able to link OEO's objectives to those of Negro citizens. However, the civil rights movement of the late 1960's was suffering dwindling support from the white majority—a trend which intensified the problems faced by federal programs associated with the movement. As long as OEO insisted on full participation by Negroes in its programs, it fell prey to resentment from southern local politicians and their representatives in Congress. In turn, southern delegations in Congress wield disproportionate influence because of their high seniority and command of key committee posts.

A corollary of the political position of the poor is of related significance; programs aimed at alleviating poverty are likely to produce increased political participation by the poor. Such participation creates pressures upon established political leaders and may even generate hostility toward poverty programs. Articulate and activist representatives of the poor are bound to clash with merchants, landlords, welfare officials, and politicians.

In many communities, northern as well as southern, OEO's clienteles threatened to grow into "anti-establishment" political groups. Local political leaders transmitted their concerns to their Congressmen who, especially within the Democratic party, were sensitive to challenges to the party's big-city base of power. Thus, the war on poverty's skirmishes with the political establishment were in some measure a gauge of its success in fulfilling its mission.

The Mississippi Head Start program, the most highly charged political controversy to confront Head Start officials, raised the question of whether OEO would support a successful project when political controversy was involved. In the summer of 1965, OEO granted $1.5 million to the Child Development Group of Mississippi (CDGM) to conduct Head Start Centers for more than 6,000 children in 28 counties. OEO showered praise on the project and, in February 1966, granted CDGM $5.6 million for a year-round project. Nevertheless, in September, OEO decided that it would not refund CDGM and later announced that it would support instead a newly-founded bi-racial group, the Mississippi Action for Progress (MAP). The new group was supported by the Mississippi governor, and its Board of Directors included the head of the Mississippi NAACP, a liberal Mississippi editor, and several business leaders.

Few proponents of Head Start questioned the effectiveness of CDGM. Their views were possibly best summed up by Dr. Robert Coles, a Harvard University research psychiatrist: "If we are fighting a war against poverty then this program is actually reaching the poor children and doing so in a way that makes any doctor feel truly impressed." This view was apparently shared by OEO officials. Even after the agency decided to cut off the project, Jule Sugarman, then Associate Director of Head Start, was reported to have admitted that, "There were more poor involved than in any program I know of." [74] He added, however, that, "Many were not directly concerned. They were not parents, and their interests were only peripherally concerned with the children." This was undoubtedly the crux of the problem, for it was known that many of the participants in CDGM were civil rights activists. Questions were also raised about CDGM's "fiscal responsibility" though apparently no malfeasance was involved—just poor bookkeeping found in many CAA projects where inexperienced administrators are not accustomed to General Accounting Office procedures.

It was no secret that the Mississippi Congressional delegation was unhappy with CDGM. And, as a member of the Senate Appropriations Committee, Senator John Stennis filed a list of charges and launched an investigation of CDGM. Advocates of the project charged that OEO's failure to renew CDGM was the consequence of these outside criticisms, a charge categorically denied by Shriver. OEO insisted that it could not,under the law, authorize additional expenditures for CDGM as long as its accounting procedures were under question and its funds may have been spent for unauthorized activities. Determined that he could not continue funding CDGM, Shriver claimed that he channeled funds to MAP to provide Head Start facilities for the children. ". . . the plight of Mississippi children," he wrote, "is more important to me than the status of any single organization." [75]

CDGM supporters—including many ardent supporters of OEO—were not persuaded by Shriver's disclaimers and began to pressure the agency to renew its support. In December 1966, OEO announced an "agreement in principle" that it would renew CDGM support, and a month later a $4.9 million grant was made to the project. [76] The new grant made the following stipulations: six of the 19 CDGM Board of Directors would be white; surveillance of operations would be maintained by an outside organization, the Board of National Missions; and employees of CDGM would not engage in partisan political activities. One can only speculate whether OEO would have renewed the grant in the absence of outside pressures, though at no time had it foreclosed this possibility. OEO did not escape unscathed, however. Civil rights advocates were embittered by what seemed a compromise with segregationists, while segregationists continued to resent OEO's financing a project associated with civil rights activists.

OEO found itself pulled in opposite directions. On the one hand, increasingly militant reformers were demanding a radical shake-up of existing political and social service practices. On the other hand, established political groups were alternatively responsive and hostile. The more members of disadvantaged groups who were brought to the threshold of political participation, the greater the potential impact upon established leaders. To the extent that OEO insisted on, for example, "maximum feasible participation" or racial integration in its programs, it encountered hostility from City Hall and Congress. To the extent that it yielded to political realities and compromised, it faced rejection by the militants. On a thousand different battlegrounds, OEO found itself in an unenviable stance in the middle.

In addition, OEO could count on the opposition of many traditionally conservative groups which viewed with horror any genuine "war on poverty." Conservative opposition was not alleviated by the fact that some of OEO's supporters—including Congressman Adam Clayton Powell—preferred to label the antipoverty programs as partisan Democratic efforts. Some Republicans, for example, were genuinely interested in supporting a bipartisan antipoverty effort; but their support was usually spurned by Democratic Congressional leaders. Resenting the exclusion, these Republicans repaid in kind by attacking OEO.

Other factors conspired to endanger OEO's support on Capitol Hill. The Education and Labor Committee, charged with responsibility for antipoverty legislation in the House, has in recent years been a divided and highly partisan committee lacking strong leadership. Its chairman in the 88th and 89th Congress was Adam Clayton Powell, whose espousal of antipoverty legislation was not calculated to win new friends for the programs. Moreover, Powell's support was inconsistent; at times he attacked OEO bitterly, appearing to be more interested in preserving his own Harlem leadership than in advancing OEO's interests. OEO's own Congressional liaison work also ran into difficulties. During OEO's first three years, four men held the post of Director of Congressional Relations. This office took upon itself the virtually impossible task of handling all Congressional inquiries, in addition to essential lobbying on Capitol Hill. The resultant bottleneck led to complaints from Senators and Representatives that their inquiries were being ignored.

From OEO's point of view, the cultivation of goodwill on Capitol Hill demanded an excessive amount of the agency's time and energies. In addition to responding to large numbers of requests for information, OEO's Congressional liaison staff—not to mention other officials—devoted an inordinate amount of time to lobbying or testifying on Capitol Hill. Beyond the annual appropriations process which most federal agencies must face, OEO had to gain renewed authorization of the basic legislation each year. In the process Congress managed to chip away so. the original flexibility given to OEO by the Act. Althc. ou Congress left OEO structurally intact (except for work-study and adult education), it curtailed the agency's freedom to allocate funds among the various programs—especially in connection with CAP. It can only be concluded that Congress did not help OEO to plan ahead or operate at maximum efficiency.

Congressional review and oversight of OEO's work during the first three years of the Act was, moreover, dominated by narrow political motivations and revealed little understanding of program contents and direction. The 1967 hearing and floor debates, however, displayed increased sophistication on the part of many legislators; and the investigation mounted that year by Senator Joseph S. Clark's Subcommittee on Employment, Manpower and Poverty represented a careful and competent review of the programs. The Subcommittee's efforts were directed by Howard W. Hallman.

OEO's political problems were endemic and pervasive. It would be impossible to detail all the issues which arose during OEO's first three years of operation. Perhaps the most useful way of understanding OEO's political context is to describe in some detail the circumstances surrounding the 1967 renewal of the Economic Opportunity Act. Many political forces converged on OEO that year, and there was even doubt that the agency would be permitted to continue. The result, as will be seen, was a controversial compromise which assured the continuation of the agency—at least for the foreseeable future.

On December 11, 1967, the House of Representatives extended the Economic Opportunity Act for a period of two years and with fewer substantive changes than anticipated. [77] The vote of 247-149 was the greatest show of strength for the Act since its passage in 1964. Sixty-four Republicans—two of every five—strayed from their usual party position to join 183 Democrats (including 38 southerners) to vote in favor of the Act. The final vote on EOA appropriations was even more lopsided—308-78.

The outcome was a surprise to most observers, for OEO was in serious political trouble. Because of their pessimism over the outcome, House Democratic leaders postponed final action until the closing days of the session. Two months before the House vote, Representative Sam Gibbons, floor leader of the 1966 EOA debate, is reported to have stated, "I have checked. The outcome is really dismal . . . there will be better than 230 negative votes on any antipoverty bill we write." [78] On two earlier occasions, a majority of House members had expressed displeasure with OEO. In an unusual step, they voted in October to exclude OEO employees from the general salary increase granted to government employees. Later in the same month, they refused to pass a "continuing resolution" authorizing OEO funds to operate at the previous year's level. For a short period between October 23 and November 9, OEO had no money and was forced to discontinue expiring projects.

There was no simple explanation for the change that took place in the House during the two months following Congressman Gibbons' count. Indeed, several forces that were eventually to influence fourscore Congressmen to vote for extending EOA were already in operation when Gibbons surveyed the mood of Congress. The House's petulant action in denying the 3,000 OEO employees their salary increase generated sympathy for the agency both in and out of Congress. The failure of Congress to pass the "continuing resolution" had a more decisive effect, for it was soon felt in a number of communities. As projects were terminated and local jobs lost, Congressmen began to hear from their constituents. Because a number of popular Head Start projects were imperiled, Congressional inaction provided a ready-made issue for attracting sympathy for the antipoverty effort—an OEO count found no less than 450 newspaper editorials during October and November favoring the continuation of EOA—and a basis for attacking the "reckless irresponsibility" of Congress. These events followed closely the much publicized defeat of the "rat bill" under which many Congressmen were still smarting. During the debate on that bill, opponents displayed a sick humor in arguing against the legislation, a fact which was widely denounced by the news media. Later the House of Representatives reversed itself and took a position against rodents, but too late to save itself from public criticism.

The Republicans had tactical reasons for opposing the continuing resolution and excluding OEO employees from the federal wage increase. They hoped to convince OEO supporters that there was not enough support in the House for extending the EOA, and that passage would require acceptance of Republican amendments. These signals were overlooked by the news media, however, and the message the public received was merely that the Republicans and some of their Democratic colleagues were against the antipoverty legislation. Though the "overkill" of OEO backfired, proponents of the agency still had to break the Republican-southern coalition which had been working effectively in the 90th Congress. Economy in social legislation was the watchword, and a majority in the House still opposed the Administration antipoverty bill with its proposed $2.06 billion authorization. Since too many members had publicly opposed it, an alternative to the Administration bill was needed.

The alternative was an amendment supplied by Representative Edith Green, an advocate of the antipoverty efforts but a persistent critic of OEO. Mrs. Green sought to limit Shriver's authority to permit private non-profit organizations to operate as community action agencies. Without passing judgment on the heated debate concerning the potential impact that may result from the changes adopted by Congress, the Green amendment provided northern Democrats a selling point with their southern colleagues. They claimed that the amendment would put the antipoverty legislation in the hands of local elected officials. The amendment apparently satisfied southern Democrats, for many moved to side with their northern colleagues rather than cooperate with the opposition.

To sustain the impression that the Green amendment meant a radical change in the administration and direction of community action programs, OEO spokesmen were persuaded to denounce the amendment as signaling the death knell of Community Action Agencies. While some OEO officials strongly opposed the amendment and needed no persuasion, others privately supported the amendment and shed crocodile tears about the supposed demise of CAP. The tactics proved effective in solidifying Congressional support for the amendment; southerners who had formerly denounced community action efforts as the work of "power-grasping bureaucrats from Washington" could now vote for the new program. [79]

Given this face-saving device, many southerners were receptive to the appeals of Congressman Carl D. Perkins, the new chairman of the House Education and Labor Committee. Having obtained the Green amendment, Perkins told his southern colleagues that they could hardly let him down and defeat the antipoverty program, leaving him open to the charge that he could not do as well for the poor as his predecessor, Adam Clayton Powell. According to a South Carolina Congressman: "I never heard his name mentioned but I know that a lot of southerners were thinking unconsciously of Powell. . . .We didn't want to pull the rug out from under Carl." [80]

The mobilization of businessmen, mayors, and other city officials to lobby for OEO also helped make it respectable to vote for the extension of the Economic Opportunity Act. OEO officials also lobbied intensively for the legislation, but it is not known how persuasive they were.

With this rare display of Democratic unity, the Republicans were unable to split the Democratic ranks with an attractive alternative. Most Republicans agreed that they could not afford the blame for killing the Act, even if they could get the votes to achieve this end. And many opposed its outright defeat, hoping rather to change it more to their liking. The major Republican spokesmen on the issue, Charles E. Goodell of New York and Albert H. Quie of Minnesota, did not seek a coalition with the southern Democrats. They concentrated their efforts on getting approval of substantive amendments to transform the program along the lines proposed in their Opportunity Crusade. Quie explained later, "I was caught . . . between two differing views—those in the Administration who simply wanted to continue the present program . . . and those of us who wanted to greatly strengthen the antipoverty program. . . ." [81] Goodell went out of his way to antagonize southern Democrats by charging that the Green provision was the "bosses and boll weevil amendment."

Whatever the substantive merits of the Opportunity Crusade, Goodell and Quie had little that was politically attractive to offer the Democrats. Their proposal would have transferred several EOA programs, including Head Start, to the Office of Education. This agency was headed by Harold Howe, II, who was anathema to the southerners because he had tried to enforce the antisegregation provisions of the Elementary and Secondary Education Act and other education legislation. Northern Democrats who might have found attractive provisions in the Opportunity Crusade were not about to do business with Republicans if they could get a majority to pass an Administration bill, and they did not consider the Green amendment too high a price to pay. Many northern Democrats, closely associated with Democratic city machines, saw nothing wrong in a "bosses" amendment, even if "boll weevils" were also involved.

The Republicans found themselves not only a minority, but a divided one. A few favored the Administration bill, and two Republicans on the House Education and Labor Committee deserted their party to vote with the majority in reporting the committee bill. A larger group—which included most of the Republican leaders in the House—cared little about the substantive amendments offered by their colleagues in the Opportunity Crusade, but were preoccupied with cutting antipoverty funds. Had the Republicans closed ranks, they might have been able to attract enough Democratic votes to pass some of their amendments. Among their numerous defeats, the House Republican leadership scored one victory by cutting funds on the antipoverty legislation. By deserting Quie and Goodell and siding with economy-minded southerners, the Republican leaders were able to cut the authorization from $2.06 billion proposed by the Administration to $1.6 billion. The final appropriation approved by Congress was $1.773 billion, only slightly less than the amount Shriver had indicated as the bare minimum if OEO was to operate for the balance of the year without cutting major projects. [82]

Footnotes

[64] Erwin Knoll and Jules Witcover, "Maximum Feasible Publicity: The War on Poverty's Campaign to Capture the Press," *Columbia Journalism Review,* Fall 1966, p. 40.

[65] Section 602 (i). The agency was explicitly exempted from the normal statutory restrictions on public information functions by federal agencies (United States Code, section 4154 of title 39).

[66] See Footnote 64, p. 34.

[67] See Footnote 5, Senate Report 563, p. 193.

[68] See Footnote 64, p. 35.

[69] Republican National Committee Press Release, July 8, 1966, p. 1 (italics in original). The GOP report, entitled, "The Alleviation of Poverty," was prepared by its Task Force on the Functions of Federal, State, and Local Governments, a group chaired by Congressman Robert Taft, Jr., of Ohio.

70 OEO Press Release, July 8, 1966.

71 Willard Edwards, "OEO Uses Poverty Funds to Belittle GOP, Ford Says," *Chicago Tribune,* July 14, 1966.

72 U.S. Congress, House Committee on Education and Labor, *Economic Opportunity Act Amendments of 1967, Hearing,* 90th Cong., 1st Sess., (Washington: Government Printing Office, 1967) Part 2, pp. 874-5, 880-1.

73 John Kenneth Galbraith, *The Affluent Society* (Boston: Houghton-Mifflin, 1958), p. 328.

74 Quoted in Patrick Young, "Why There's A Big Fuss in a Pre-School Program," *National Observer,* October 10, 1966.

75 Letter of Sargent Shriver, "Shriver Defends Mississippi Action," *The New York Times,* October 25, 1966.

76 OEO Press Release, "OEO Announces CDGM Head Start Grant," January 30, 1967.

77 Joseph A. Loftus, "How the Poverty Bill Was Saved in the House," *The New York Times,* December 25, 1967.

78 William C. Selover, "Antipoverty Program Stumbles in Congress," *The Christian Science Monitor,* October 12, 1967.

79 Richard L. Lyons, "City Hall Amendment Key to OEO Victory," *The Washington Post,* November 19, 1967.

80 William Greider, "Poverty Bill Boosts Perkins' Esteem," *Courier-Journal,* November 21, 1967.

81 Guest Editorial by Rep. Albert H. Quie, Rochester, Minnesota *Post-Bulletin,* January 13, 1968.

82 Joseph W. Sullivan, "House GOP 'Activism' Takes a Drubbing," *Wall Street Journal,* November 17, 1967; Tom Littlewood, "Poverty Bill Fight Highlights Rivalry in the GOP," *Chicago Sun-Times,* November 19, 1967.

THE FUTURE
OF OEO

An obvious question for the future of OEO is whether the two-year extension should be interpreted as an end of the annual crises or merely as a temporary reprieve. The answer is not at all clear.

OEO was not allowed much of a respite. One of the 1967 amendments to the Act (introduced by Senator Winston L. Prouty of Vermont) directed the General Accounting Office to investigate the poverty programs "in sufficient depth," not only to evaluate their effectiveness but also to enable the Comptroller General to make "recommendations for additional legislation. . . ." The report was due by December 1, 1968, and GAO was therefore breathing down OEO's neck for the entire year. An objective evaluation of OEO should be helpful, however, not only to help Congress determine the future direction of the Act, but also to allow OEO to take stock of its performance during the first four years.

After Congress completed action, a leading sponsor of the Opportunity Crusade declared that the Republican alternative was dead. This does not mean that other alternatives could not be developed. As long as the war on poverty remains a series of fragmented programs, some administered by OEO and some delegated, there will remain ample opportunities to spin off OEO-operated programs to agencies with established jurisdictions in the various fields. There is ample precedent for this. The college-level work-study program was transferred to the Office of Education during the Act's first year; the small business loan program, although it remains part of the Act, is administered almost completely independently of OEO. In addition, new agencies may be developed which would be logical depositories for EOA activities. On the drawing board is a proposal to create a new Department of Education and Manpower. Should this proposed department materialize, it would no doubt absorb many antipoverty programs, possibly most of them.

Transfer of antipoverty activities will not have to await the creation of a new department if Congresswoman Edith Green has her way. Mrs. Green, who chairs the House Subcommittee on General Education, announced her intention to try to transfer some OEO programs to other agencies. A Republican majority of the House would strengthen the forces favoring changes in jurisdiction and administration, including the disbanding of OEO and transferal of its coordinating responsibilities as proposed by the Opportunity Crusade. A prime candidate for spin off is Upward Bound, a $30 million program which helps bright students from poor homes to enter college. A similar program, Talent Search, is administered by the Office of Education. Head Start is also a candidate for transfer, if southern opposition to the Office of Education diminishes or if Commissioner Howe leaves. The transfer or phasing out of Job Corps continues to be discussed, and OEO has already been forced to close sixteen centers—out of 123—because of cuts in Job Corps funds.

Of course, the immediate course of the war on poverty depends upon the course of the other war being fought in Vietnam. Originally it was assumed that spending for the antipoverty efforts would have to rise rapidly, as localities geared up for participation in the programs. In fact, spending for Economic Opportunity Act programs has not, as it turned out, grown nearly as fast as the planning or needs required. And after 1965, with the nation becoming more deeply involved in Vietnam, domestic programs like those under the Act were simply prevented from major upward changes in the level of spending. Any evaluation of OEO must therefore recognize that OEO was not given a fighting chance to attack the problem of poverty. And any speculation about OEO's future must turn upon the nation's resolve to place higher priority upon this most important war.

The future of OEO at the local level is even less clear. Recent trends have bolstered community action agencies by assigning them greater responsibility in the administration of expanding manpower programs. However, placing CAA's under the control of local officials may lead to spinning off programs at the local level. No doubt the picture will be mixed, and the scope of local CAA's will vary widely as in the past. In many communities the local antipoverty agencies have established their own clientele and support; and in such cases, elected officials are unlikely to impinge upon the jurisdiction of the CAA's.

All these dire alternatives for the future of OEO may come to naught. If OEO follows the usual pattern, it could well be removed from the center of attention and controversy and become part of the American scene. Other welfare programs could attract greater attention and relegate OEO to the background. The center of the stage might be assumed by income maintenance programs, whether negative income tax, family allowance or related schemes. It is not likely that the functions of the OEO will disappear in the foreseeable future, but the programs may become part of the federal establishment and share relative obscurity with scores of other efforts.

OTHER INSTITUTE PUBLICATIONS

DOCUMENT AND REFERENCE TEXT (DART). An Index
to Minority Group Employment Information. Computer-generated DART
Index lists 5000 documents dealing with minority group employment and
related problems in full-title KWIC format.   650 pp. $22.50

INDEX TO POVERTY, HUMAN RESOURCES AND MANPOWER INFORMATION. KWIC and KWOC format provides
direct access to major writings of the 1960's in this field. 1500 bibliographic
entries, cross-referenced by author, subject and title.   508 pp. $20.00

CONFERENCE ON AUTOMATION, FULL EMPLOYMENT AND A BALANCED ECONOMY. Papers presented at
the Rome Conference of 1967 includes articles by Jirkowicz, Crossley,
Meidner, Barnes, Moberg, Haber, Weber, Strender, Roberts, Dunlop, Marsh,
Kellgren, Barkin and Flanders.   2.50

POVERTY AND HUMAN RESOURCES ABSTRACTS (PHRA). Published six times a year, each issue of PHRA contains 200
abstracts drawn from publications of government agencies and private
foundations; major journals, periodicals and books; unpublished papers
and conference reports; and literature referred by specialists on problems
of poverty, manpower and human resources. Featured in each issue is an
original article on major problems and issues of contemporary society and
a special report on the Washington scene. Each paperbound issue, published bimonthly, contains a detailed index.   Annual subscription $40.00

Address orders and inquiries to

PUBLICATIONS OFFICE

Institute of Labor and Industrial Relations
P. O. Box 1567
Ann Arbor, Michigan 48106

The Policy Papers

IN HUMAN RESOURCES AND INDUSTRIAL RELATIONS.
Established in 1967 and published on an unscheduled basis, each paper is an essay by a leading expert on a current issue or topic in human resources or industrial relations. The publication of the Policy Papers is intended to provide information and stimulate discussion on the major issues and problems of our industrial society.

Address orders and inquiries to:

Publications Office

Institute of Labor and Industrial Relations
P. O. Box 1567
Ann Arbor, Michigan 48106

Bulk rates available on request. Publisher pays handling and postage on orders accompanied by payment; orders to be billed will be charged 50¢ per order handling charges.